The New York City Charter Bill.

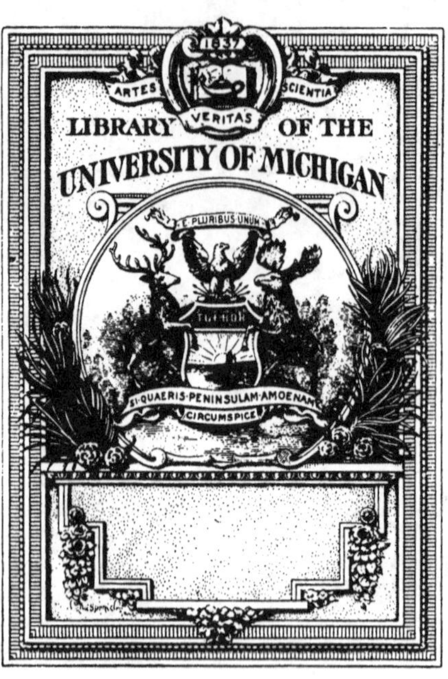
1837
ARTES
SCIENTIA
VERITAS
LIBRARY OF THE
UNIVERSITY OF MICHIGAN
E PLURIBUS UNUM
TUEBOR
SI·QUAERIS·PENINSULAM·AMOENAM
CIRCUMSPICE

THE NEW YORK CITY CHARTER BILL.

TEXT OF DIFFERENCE BETWEEN BILL AS
PROPOSED BY THE CHARTER
REVISION COMMISSION
AND
BILL AS PASSED BY LEGISLATURE
5TH APRIL, 1901.

SECOND EDITION.

PUBLISHED BY THE CITY CLUB OF NEW YORK,
12TH APRIL, 1901.

NOTE.

This pamphlet is an attempt to show the actual differences between the text of the charter bill as passed by the legislature on the 5th of April, and that of the bill as proposed by the Charter Revision Commission. It is for the information of those who desire to know what the changes are, and who have not the time for the necessary laborious comparison.

In order that this comparative statement might be published without undue delay, it has been necessary to assume generally the correctness of the marking in the printed bill as passed, designed to show the changes which the bill would make in the present charter. In view of this necessity and of the haste with which the work of comparison has been done, some inaccuracies will perhaps be found in the text here printed. The section numbers are those which the sections would bear in the charter after the enactment of the bill as passed. In a few cases of sections appearing only in the bill as proposed by the Revision Commission, the numbers are those of the section in that form of the bill.

TEXT OF PARTS OF CHARTER BILL

AS PASSED BY LEGISLATURE, 5th APRIL, 1900.

SHOWING CHANGES FROM THE FORM OF BILL AS PROPOSED BY CHARTER REVISION COMMISSION.

[All matter in brackets would be enacted into law as part of the bill in the form proposed by the Commission, but not as part of the bill as passed; all matter underlined would be enacted into law as part of the bill as passed, but not as part of the bill in the form proposed by the Commission. Matter neither bracketed nor underlined is common to the two bills. That is: the following text read with the matter in brackets and without the matter underlined, is in the form which the enactment of the Commission's bill would give the law; read with the matter underlined and without the matter in brackets, it is in the form which the enactment of the bill as passed would give the law. The words "the bill" are used to mean the bill as passed by the legislature: the words "Commission's bill" are used to mean the bill as proposed by the Charter Revision Commission.]

In section 18, relating to the board of aldermen, the only change is in the insertion of the clause underlined below:—

Any vacancy which may occur among the members elected to the board of aldermen shall be filled by election by a majority of all the members elected thereto, of a person who must be of the same political party as the member whose place has become vacant; and the person so elected to fill any such vacancy shall serve for the unexpired portion of the term.

Section 19 in the bill defines seventy-three aldermanic districts, from each of which, under the provision of section 18, one alderman would be elected every two years. The bill does not provide for the making of any change in the aldermanic district from time to time. Section 19 in the Commission's bill defines a hundred and twenty-three aldermanic districts into which the city would be divided, and from each of which an alderman would be elected every two years. Upon each re-apportionment of assembly districts the board of aldermen "shall " increase or diminish the number of such districts, so that there shall " always be two aldermanic districts for every assembly district lying " wholly within the City of New York."

Id., police, health, park, fire and building regulations.

§43. The board of aldermen shall have power to make, establish, alter, modify, amend and repeal all ordinances, rules, and police, health park, fire and building regulations, not contrary to the laws of the state, or the United States, as they may deem necessary to carry into effect the powers conferred upon The City of New York by this act, or by any other law of the state, or by grant; and such as they may deem necessary and proper for the good government, order and protection of persons and property, and for the preservation of the public health, peace and prosperity of said city and its inhabitants, except so far as power is conferred by this act upon presidents of boroughs, the police, health, park, and fire departments respectively to make rules for the government of the persons employed in and by said departments. Nothing in this section contained shall be construed to impair the powers conferred by this act upon the department of education; and except so far as the legislative power respecting the health, police, park, fire and building departments shall be conferred upon said departments respectively by the provisions of this act, and except that any modification of the existing rules, regulations and ordinances affecting any of the departments and all ordinances to be passed to govern the board of public improvements or any of the departments thereof, must originate with the department concerned, or with said board, and must be adopted or rejected by the board of aldermen without amendment.

From section 48:—

The action of the board of aldermen in passing any such proposition or franchise, whether by an affirmative vote, or by a failure of a majority of all the members of the board of aldermen to vote against the same, shall be subject to the approval of the mayor and to the action of the board of aldermen in case of a veto, as provided in [section forty of] this act.

From section 51:—

Subject to the constitution and the laws of the state, the board of aldermen shall have power to provide for the licensing and otherwise regulating the business of dirt carts, public cartmen, truckmen, hackmen, cabmen, expresssmen car drivers and boatmen; of boot-blacks; of pawnbrokers, junk-dealers, keepers of intelligence offices, dealers in second hand articles, hawkers, peddlers, vendors and scalpers in coal freights; of menageries, circuses and common shows; of bone boiling, fat rendering and other noxious businesses; and shall have power to regulate or forbid the keeping of dogs.

[Licenses to run omnibuses, etc.

Section 53. The board of aldermen shall have power to authorize the establishment, operation or extension of any right for the running of stages or omnibuses, whether operated by horses or by other motive power, and to license and regulate such stages and omnibuses. Every proposition for a license to maintain or operate a line of stages or omnibuses, or to extend an existing line, or to change the motive power, shall be referred by the board of aldermen to the board of estimate and apportionment, who shall, after due inquiry, recommend such terms and conditions for granting the same as in their judgment will best protect the interests of the city and the travelling public. It shall be one of the conditions of granting any such license that the person operating the same shall pay annually into the city treasury for the first five years after commencing operations thereunder five per cent. of the gross receipts of the entire route, and shall pay into the city treasury annually after the expiration of such five years, seven per cent. of such gross receipts. No such license shall be granted by the board of aldermen except on terms and conditions approved by the board of estimate and apportionment. No such license shall be granted for any longer period than twenty-five years; but the ordinance granting such license may provide, upon payment of an increased percentage to be fixed therein, for giving the grantee a renewal for a further period of not more than twenty-five years. Upon the adoption of an ordinance by the board of aldermen granting a license as in this section provided, the route may be maintained and operated in accordance therewith, and the ownership of such route may be transferred. No license granted under this section shall confer any exclusive right or privilege unless the consent in writing, duly acknowledged, of the owners of a majority of the property in each of the streets along the proposed route shall have been obtained and filed with the board of aldermen before the adoption of the ordinance granting such license.]

From section 56:—

It shall be the duty of the board of aldermen, upon the recommendation of the board of estimate and apportionment, to fix the salary of every officer or person whose compensation is paid out of the city treasury other than day laborers, and teachers, examiners and members of the supervising staff of the department of education, irrespective of the amount fixed by this act, except that no change shall be made in the salary of an elected officer or head of a department during his tenure of office.

Private rights protected.

§ 85. This grant shall not impair or affect any existing valid private rights, or the existing riparian rights of owners of private property, or the lawful rights of private owners of docks, piers and other structures in the said city or any part thereof.

From section 94:—

The mayor shall be the chief executive officer of the city; he shall be elected at the general election in the year nineteen hundred and one and every [four] two years thereafter, and shall hold his office for the term of [four] two years commencing at noon on the first day of January after his election. [He shall be ineligible for the next term after the termination of his office.] The salary of the mayor shall be fifteen thousand dollars a year.

From section 95:—

The mayor may, whenever in his judgment the public interests shall so require, remove from office any public officer holding office by appointment from a mayor of The City of New York, except members of the board of education and aqueduct commissioners, trustees of the College of The City of New York, and trustees of Bellevue and allied hospitals, and except also judicial offices for whose removal other provision is made by the constitution. No public officer shall hold his office for any specific term, except as in this act is otherwise expressly provided.

In the list of administrative departments in section 96 is added the "Tenement house department."

From section 97:—

The head of the department of finance shall be called the comptroller of The City of New York. He shall be elected at the general election in the year [eighteen hundred and ninety-seven] nineteen hundred and one, and every [four] two years thereafter, and shall hold his office for the term of [four] two years, commencing at noon on the first day of January, after his election.

From section 106:—

§ 106. The head of the department of docks and ferries shall be called the commissioner [board] of docks. [Said board shall consist of three members, who shall be known as commissioners of docks.]

Tenement house department.

§ 110. The head of the tenement house department shall be called the tenement house commissioner. He shall be appointed by the mayor, and shall, unless sooner removed, hold his office for six years, and until his successor shall be appointed and has qualified.

Sections 111 and 112 in the bill are, respectively, sections 110 and 111 in the Commission's bill.

[Bureau of municipal statistics and records.

§ 128. There shall be a bureau of municipal statistics and records of The City of New York.]

[Bureau ; how constituted.

§ 129. The bureau of municipal statistics and records shall consist of a commissioner of statistics and records and of such assistants as may be found necessary for properly carrying on the work of the bureau.]

[Commissioner of statistics and records to be appointed by the mayor.

§ 130. The commissioner of statistics and records shall be appointed by the mayor.

[Compensation of Commissioner of statistics and records.

§ 134. The commissioner of statistics and records shall receive an annual salary of three thousand five hundred dollars.]

[Power and duties of the commissioner in relation to the collection and publication of statistics.

§ 135. The commissioner shall devise and carry out plans for the collection and publication of such statistical data relating to the city as shall be deemed of utility or interest to the officials and citizens of the city. The head of each department of the city shall, upon a request from the commissioner made through the mayor, and approved by him, transmit to the commissioner for his use, upon such blanks as may be provided, or in such other manner as may be deemed convenient by the commissioner, such statistical data relating to the work of such department as the commissioner may call for. The commissioner of statistics and records shall publish annually, with the approval of the board of estimate and apportionment, a volume to be known as the "Municipal statistics of The City of New York for the year * * *" In this volume the commissioner shall publish, in so far as he may deem advisable, the results attending the work of the various departments of the city government for the preceding calendar year, and such other statistical information and facts relating to The City of New York or its inhabitants as he may deem of general public interest. Such publication shall contain statistics relating to population and births, marriages and deaths; to streets, pavements, sewers, markets, docks, parks, buildings, fires, water supply and sanitary condition of the city; to the administration of charities and corrections, of the police department, of the various branches of the judiciary and the criminal courts of the city; to the work of the department of education, the number of children of school age and those attending school; to municipal revenues and expenditures, the administration of the various city departments having charge of the expenditure of public moneys, the collection of taxes and the management of the city debt; and also a general statement of the legislative enactments relating to the government of The City of New York.]

[Powers and duties of the commissioner in relation to the collection and preservation of records.]

[§ 136. It shall be the duty of the commissioner of statistics and records to collect, preserve and make properly accessible the manuscript records of The City of New York. By these are meant all journals, minute books, maps and plans, files of papers, parchments and documents of public character which relate to the history of The City of New York, and to all departments of the same, since its incorporation as a municipality; also the records, similarly defined, of all the cities, towns and villages whlch at any time have been annexed to or consolidated with The City of New York and which are now extinct jurisdictions. He shall have the authority and it shall be his duty to recover such of these records as may be in private hands, and to institute search for such as appear to be lost; also to procure from the city clerk and from the heads ot city departments, or other officials, the records now in their custody which fall within the meaning of this clause. But no official or head of department shall be required to surrender to said commissioner any book, document or paper which is less than twenty years old, or which he shall certify to be necessary for the trunsaction of current business in his office. Of the books, papers and documents thus accumulated the commissioner of statistics and records shall be the sole and lawful custodian. It shall be the duty of the commissioner to preserve the said records in adequate, fireproof rooms, provided and furnished at the expense of the city, and located as near as may be to the repository of the records of the county of New York. Such records shall be kept in such manner and under such regulations that they may at all proper times be accessible to those who desire to consult them. He shall cause proper shelves, cases and files to be provided for them, and shall, as may be needed, cause them to be bound, copied, arranged and indexed.]

[Limitation of expense of maintaining the bureau of statistics and records.

137. The expense of such publications and all other expenses of the bureau of statistics and records, shall be included in the annual budget. The total expense of maintaining the bureau of statistics and records, including salaries, shall not exceed in any one year the sum of fifteen

thousand dollars, unless otherwise provided by the board of estimate and apportionment and the board of aldermen.]

From section 163:—

Any farmer or market gardener, or dealer in farm or garden produce, desiring to use such market, or the market in the borough of Brooklyn known as the Wallabout farmers' market, may present to the department of finance an affidavit, stating his name, residence, occupation and a general description of the commodities which he desires to sell in any such market, together with a request that a license be issued to him to use the same.

From section 216:—

It shall not be lawful for The City of New York to make or cause to be made any alteration of rates or charges affecting any item or source of the revenues of any of the sinking funds of said city, or of the general fund which may tend to a diminution of the receipts from such source of revenue, or either of them, except that it shall be lawful for The City of New York to exempt places of public worship from the payment of any fee for the construction of vaults under the sidewalk or in front thereof, and all the revenues of said corporation not by law otherwise specifically appropriated, shall, when received into the city treasury, be credited to the general fund.

From section 230:—

[Fourth—The sum of ten thousand dollars to the credit of the department of health, to be known as the tenement house fund, to be expended by the board of health.]

Other changes in numbers of paragraphs in section 230 result from this omission.

[Authority to change the map or plan of the city or to change grades.

Section 243. The board of estimate and apportionment is authorized and empowered, whenever and as often as it may deem it for the public interest so to do, to initiate a change in the map or plan of The City of New York, so as to lay out new streets, parks, bridges, tunnels and approaches to bridges, and tunnels and parks, and to widen, straighten, extend, alter and close existing streets, and to change the grade of existing streets shown upon such map or plan, by publishing notice of its proposed action for ten days in the City Record, and the corporation newspapers, and giving an opportunity for all persons interested in such change to be heard at a time and place to be specified in such notice, such time to be not less than ten days after the publication of such notice. After the due publication of such notice, and after hearing protests and objections if any there be, against the proposed change, if the said board shall favor such change, notwithstanding such protests and objections, it shall transmit its resolutions to that effect to the board of aldermen, together with the objections, if any, which have been made in writing, and filed with it, and a statement of its reasons for such determination. If the board of aldermen concur in such resolution passed by the board of estimate and apportionment, by passing an ordinance adopting and approving the same by a two-thirds vote, and the same receives the approval of the mayor, such change in the map or plan of The City of New York, or in the grade of any street or streets shown thereon, shall be deemed to have been made. The board of estimate and apportionment is authorized and empowered without the concurrence of the board of aldermen, but with the approval of the mayor, to change the grades of bridges, tunnels and approaches to bridges and tunnels, and the location of approaches to bridges and tunnels.]

From section 255, relating to the corporation counsel:—

He shall not permit, offer or confess judgment against the city, or accept any offer of judgment in favor of the city [or determine not to take an appeal, or abandon an appeal already taken] without the previous written approval of the comptroller; and in case of any claim for a money judgment exceeding ten thousand dollars, or for relief other than in the nature of a money judgment, the previous written approval of the mayor shall be also necessary.

From section 259, relating to the bureau for the recovery of penalties:—

The assistant corporation counsel assigned to this bureau in the main office, or in the branch office located in any borough, subject only to the approval of the corporation counsel, may settle, compromise, adjust, or discontinue, any action brought to recover a penalty in the name of The City of New York or any department, board, bureau, or officer thereof, provided that the penalty sued for does not exceed the sum of one hundred dollars.

Police commissioner; salary; deputies; salaries, etc.

§ 270. The head of the police department shall be called the police commissioner, who shall be appointed by the mayor, and shall, [hold office as provided in chapter four of this act] unless sooner removed, hold office for the term of five years, and until his successor shall be appointed and has qualified. The said commissioner may, whenever, in the judgment of the mayor of said city or the governor, the public interest shall so require, be removed from office by either, and shall be ineligible for reappointment thereto. The successors in office of the said commissioner shall also be appointed by the mayor of the city within ten days after any vacancy shall occur, and shall be removed by either the mayor or governor whenever the public interest so require. [The terms of office of the members of the police board, except the president thereof appointed pursuant to the provisions of the Greater New York charter, shall cease and determine on the first day of January, nineteen hundred and two, and the president of the police board shall thereupon become the police commissioner.]

The salary of said police commissioner shall be [ten thousand] seventy-five hundred dollars a year. The said commissioner shall have the power to appoint, from the citizens of the United States and residents of the said city, and at pleasure remove, two deputies, to be known as first deputy commissioner and second deputy commissioner; the first deputy commissoner, shall, during the absence or disability of the commissioner, possess all the powers and perform all the duties of the commissioner except the power of making appointments and transfers. In the absence or disability of both the commissioner and the first deputy commissioner; the second deputy commissioner shall possess all the powers and perform all the duties of the commissioner except the power of making appointments and transfers. The commissioner shall define the duties of the deput[ies]y commissioners, and may delegate to either of them any of his powers except the power of making appointments and transfers. The salary of each of such deput[ies]y commissioners shall be four thousand dollars a year.

Police commissioner; authority; bureau of elections.

§ 271. The said police commissioner shall have cognizance and control of the government, administration, disposition and discipline of the said police department and of the police force of said department [and it shall also have cognizance and control of the bureau of elections hereinafter mentioned and said bureau of elections shall be a part of said police department.]

Police force; composition.

§ 276. Until otherwise provided by the board of aldermen, upon the recommendation of the mayor and the police commissioner, the police force in the police department created by this chapter shall consist of the following members, to wit: [A chief of police; two deputy chiefs of police;] Fifteen inspectors of police; captains of police, not exceeding in number one to each fifty of the total number of patrolmen, except in the rural portion of the city; sergeants of police, not exceeding four in number to each fifty of the total number of patrolmen; roundsmen not exceeding four in number to each fifty patrolmen; detective sergeants to the number authorized by law; the members of the telegraph force as specified in section two hundred and seventy-seven of this act the superintendent and inspectors of boilers as specified in scction three hundred and forty-two of this act; doormen of police, not exceeding two in number to each fifty of the total number of patrolmen; surgeons of police, not exceeding forty in number, one of whom shall be chief surgeon, and patrolmen to the number of six thousand three hundred and eighty-two. [The police commissioner shall appoint twode puty chiefs of police from among the five deputy chiefs of police in office, and the three deputy chiefs of police not so appointed.] The deputy chiefs of police who shall have been in said office prior to the time when this act shall take effect shall become inspectors of pclice, with the salaries of deputy chiefs, and the rights granted to deputy chiefs, in respcct to the relief pension fund.

From section 288 :—

[No promotion shall be made, except in the case of a vacancy in the office of chief of police, unless the same is recommended by the chief of police in writing, stating his reasons for such recommendation. In case of the rejection of any recommendation for promotion, the chief of police shall submit another name within three days, and shall continue so to do until the vacancy is filled.] * * * * * * * * * * [Deputy chiefs of police shall be elected from among inspectors who shall have served at least three years as such. The chief of police shall be appointed by the police commissioner and, if selected rom the uniformed force, he shall be appointed from among the deputy chiefs of police or inspectors who shall have served at least five years as such inspectors.]

From section 292 :—

The police commissioner [chief of police] shall be the chief executive officer of the police force. *** He shall have power to suspend without pay, pending the trial of charges, any member of the police force,[provided, however, that no such suspension shall be continued for a period of more than ten days without affirmative action to that effect by the police board.]. If any member of the police force so suspended shall not be convicted by the police commissioner of the charges so preferred, he shall be entitled to full pay from the date of suspension, notwithstanding such charges and suspension. Said [chief of] police commissioner may grant leaves of absence to members of the force for a period not exceeding five days. [He shall report to the police commissioner all changes or assignments of officers and all leaves of absence granted.]

[Id. ; Absence or disability of.

Section 293. In case of the absence or disability of the chief of police, either deputy chief of police designated by him shall discharge all the duties of the chief of police; or in case such deputy chief of police be absent or disabled, or, for any good cause, is not available for such designation, then the duties of chief of police shall be performed by one of the inspectors of police to be designated by the police commissioner.]

From section 299:—

The annual salaries and compensation of the officers and members of the police force shall be as follows, to wit: [Of the chief of police, six thousand dollars;] Of each [deputy chief of police,] inspector of police who was heretofore a deputy chief of police, as provided in section two hundred and seventy-six of this act, five thousand dollars.

From section 300:—

He shall have power and is authorized to adopt rules and regulations for the examination, hearing, investigation and determination of charges made or preferred against any member or members of said force, [except the chief of police.] * * * * * * * * [The chief of police may be removed; but only upon due trial and conviction by the mayor on the charges preferred. The police commissioner may, with the approval of the mayor, retire the chief of police or any deputy chief; but the retirement, under this provision, of a chief of police who was not at the time of his appointment a member of the uniformed force, shall not entitle him to receive any compensation by way of pension, or otherwise, from the City after his retirement.]

From section 301:—

The police commissioner, each of his deputies, [the chief of police,] each deputy of police, the chief clerk and first deputy clerk of said police department are hereby authorized and empowered to administer oaths and affirmations in the usual or appropriate forms to any person in any matter or proceedings authorized as aforesaid. * * * * * * * Any person making a complaint that a felony or misdemeanor has been committed may be required to make oath or affirmation thereto, and for this purpose [a] the police commissioner, each of his deputies [the chief of police,] the deputy chiefs of police, the chief clerk, or deputy clerks of the police department, the inspectors, captains and sergeants of police shall have power to administer oaths and affirmations.

From section 306:—

[Neither the police commissioner nor any deputy commissioner nor any] No person in the police force shall be permitted to contribute any moneys, directly or indirectly, to any political fund, or to join or be or become a member of any political club or association or any club or association intended to affect legislation for or on behalf of the police department or any member thereof, or to contribute any funds for such purpose.

Section 307:—

It shall be the duty of the [chief of] police commissioner to detail, or to cause to be detailed on election day, at least two patrolmen at each election poll.

From section 308:—

The police commissioner may, upon an emergency or apprehension of riot, tumult, mob, insurrection, pestilence or invasion, appoint as many special patrolmen without pay from among the citizens as he [it] may deem desirable. * * * * * * * * No transfer, detail or assignment to special duty of any member of the police force, except in cases authorized or required by law, shall hereafter be made or continued, except for police reasons and in the interests of police service; provided, however, that the [chief of] police commissioner may, whenever the exigencies of the case require it, make detail to special duty for a period not exceeding three days.

From section 316:—

The [chief of] police commissioner and each of his deputies and each deputy chief of police, and each inspector in his district, and each captain of police within his precinct shall possess powers of general police supervision and inspection over all licensed or unlicensed pawnbrokers, venders, junkshop keepers, junk-boatmen, cartmen, dealers in second-hand merchandise, intelligence-office keepers, and auctioneers, within the said city. * * * The said [chief of] police commissioner and each of his deputies and each deputy chief of police, and each inspector in his district and each captain within his precinct, may, by authority in writing, empower any member of the police force, whenever such member shall be in search of property feloniously obtained, or in search of suspected offenders, or evidence to convict any person charged with crime, to examine the books of any pawnbroker, or his business premises, or the business premises of any licensed vender, or licensed junk-shop keeper, or dealer in second-hand merchandise, or intelligence-office keeper, or auctioneer, or boat of any junk-boatman.

From section 317:—

The [chief of] police commissioner, each of his deputies, the [deputy chiefs of police,] inspectors of police, and captains of police and persons acting by their, or by either of their orders, shall have power to examine the books of any pawnbroker, his clerk or clerks, if they deem it necessary, when in search of stolen property, and any person having in his possession a pawnbroker's ticket shall, when accompanied by a policeman, or by an order from the [chief of] police commissioner or either of his deputies, [or a deputy chief of police,] or an inspector of police, or a captain of police, be allowed to examine the property purporting to be pawned by said ticket.

From section 318:—

If any two or more householders shall report in writing, under their signature, to the [chief of] police commissioner or to a deputy [chief of] police commissioner, that there are good grounds (and stating the same) for believing any house, room or premises within the said city to be kept or used as a common gambling-house, common gaming-room, or common gaming premises, for therein playing for wagers of money at any game of chance, or to be kept or used for lewd and obscene purposes or amusements, or the deposit or sale of lottery tickets or lottery policies, it shall be lawful for the [chief of] police commissioner or either of his deputies or a deputy chief of police to authorize, in writing, any member or members of the police force to enter the same. * * * * It shall be the duty of the said [chief of] police commissioner or deputy police commissioner or deputy chief of police to cause such arrested person to be rigorously prosecuted, and such articles seized to be destroyed, as the orders, rules and regulations of the police commissioner shall direct.

From section 357:—

Neither the police commissioner nor either deputy police commissioner shall be members of the police force within the meaning of the provisions of this act relating to pensions, nor be entitled to any pension, nor share in the relief pension fund of the police department.

From section 371 :—

§ 371. [358.] All moneys realized by sales under this chapter shall be paid over to the chamberlain of The City of New York, to the credit of the general fund of said city.

[Note :—This section should be 358 in the bill.]

From section 360 :—

In case there is no police court in close proximity to a station house in said city, then police matrons may be appointed to any station house therein.

Police Matrons to be Members of Uniform Force.

§ 360a. Such police matrons shall be regular members of the uniformed police force, and shall have the same standing in the police department and be subject to the same fines, discipline and benefits as patrolmen. They shall be provided with a suitable shield or badge of office, and shall, while on duty wear a uniform similar in color to that worn by other members of the uniformed police force. No police matron who shall become a member of the uniformed police force shall, under any pretense whatever, share in for her own benefit, any present, fee, gift, emolument for police services, or for services of the police department or any member thereof, additional to her regular salary ; and it be shall cause for removal from the police force for any matron thereof to receive any such reward or present or to receive compensation for any privilege whatever which she may grant to the women prisoners under her charge.

[Moneys paid to pension fund by matrons to be returned]—Matrons to contribute to pension fund and share therein.

§ 366. [All moneys heretofore contributed by any police matron to the pension fund of the police force shall be returned and paid back to such police matron with interest thereon from the date of such contribution, such interest to be paid by the City of New York from the contingent fund of the police department.] Every police matron upon being appointed to the uniformed force, shall, each year thereafter, and under the regulations prescribed for patrolmen, contribute two per centum of the salary received by her to the pension fund of the police force, and all fines and forfeitures imposed upon police matrons of the uniformed force, or emoluments received by them under the regulations prescribed for patrolmen, shall be contributed to the pension fund of the police force. A police matron who shall have performed duty on such police force for a period of twenty years or upward, upon her own application in writing may, or upon the certificate of so many of the police surgeons as the police board may require showing that a matron of whatever age who has served twenty years as police matron is permanently disabled physically or mentally, so as to be unfit for duty, shall, by order of the police board, be relieved and dismissed from said force and service and placed on the roll of the pension fund, and awarded and granted to be paid from said fund an annual pension during her lifetime of a sum not less than one-half of the full salary or compensation of such matron so retired. Pensions granted under this section shall be for the natural life of the pensioner and shall not be revoked or diminished. The police board shall have power in its discretion, to retire or dismiss from membership in the police force and thereupon grant a pension to any police matron who shall, after ten years and less than twenty-five years membership in any such police force become physically or mentally incapacitated for further service in the department through injuries received during the performance of her duties

§ 368-375 in the commission's bill relate to the Bureau of Elections. The sections are omitted from the bill, the subject being covered by the board of elections law recently enacted.

From section 382, relating to presidents of boroughs:—

* * The president shall hold his office for a term of [four] two years, commencing at noon on the first day of January next after his election.

From section 425:—

Districts for home rule and local improvements.

For the purposes of home rule and local improvements the territory of the City of New York is hereby divided into twenty-five districts of local improvements.

Assessments on lands used as reservoirs.

§ 480. The lands heretofore taken or to be taken for storage, reservoirs, or for other constructions necessary for the introduction and maintenance of a sufficient supply of water in the city, or for the purpose of preventing contamination or pollution, shall be assessed and taxed in the counties in which they are or may be located, in the manner prescribed by law, [at the value of the lands,] exclusive of the aqueducts, [and the construction and works necessary for its purpose provided that the assessed value of the said lands shall not exceed the assessed value of the lands in the immediate neighborhood thereof.] But nothing in this section contained shall prevent the assessors in the County of Nassau from assessing the pumping stations and buildings located in such county.

Legal effect of act upon new aqueduct.

§518. Nothing in this act contained shall be deemed or construed to repeal, or in any wise affect chapter four hundred and ninety of the laws of eighteen hundred and eighty-three, entitled "An act to provide new reservoirs, dams and a new aqueduct with the appurtenances thereto for the purpose of supplying the City of New York with an increased supply of pure and wholesome water," or the several acts amendatory thereof, but the said act and its amendments shall remain in full force and effect, [provided that the commissioners therein specified, shall not hereafter begin the construction of any new work, except such as may be properly and necessarily appurtenant to the work, the construction of which has been begun before the date upon which this act takes effect.] The term of office of the commissioners appointed and existing under the aforesaid act shall cease and determine on the completion of the work, and thereupon all papers, documents and records in possession of the aqueduct commissioners shall be delivered to the commissioner of water supply, gas and electricity.

Id.; permit necessary to take up pavement, etc.; commissioner of water supply, etc., to determine method of extension; board of aldermen may enact ordinances regulating use, etc.

§528. It shall be unlawful, after the passage of this act, for any person or corporation to take up the pavement of any of the streets, [and parks] avenues, highways or other public places of said city, or to excavate for the purpose of laying underground any electrical conductors, [or to construct] of constructing subways, or of erecting poles, unless permission in writing therefor shall have been first obtained from the said commissioner of water supply, gas and electricity with the written approval or endorsed by the commissioner of highways the president of the borough within which it is desired to lay such conduits, erect such poles, or to construct such subways. [And except with a like permission therefor no.] No electrical conductors, [poles, wires or other electrical devices or fixtures] shall be [constructed, erected,] strung, laid or maintained above or below the surface of any street, avenue, highway or other public place, in any part of said city without permission in writing from said commissioner therefor. And the said commissioner of public buildings, lighting and supplies shall determine whether any extension of the existing electrical conductors of any person or corporation in said city shall be by means of overhead or underground conductors. [And the] The board of aldermen may establish, and may from time to time enact general ordinances regulating [all] the construction, maintenance and, use and management of the electrical conductors, poles and fixtures above ground and the conduits and subways therefor constructed under ground, [and for regulating the number and location of overhead lines].

From section 536 : —

Neither the commissioner of street cleaning, nor any deputy commissioner of street cleaning, nor any member of the uniformed force of the street cleaning department, shall be permitted to contribute any moneys, directly or indirectly, to any political fund, or [to join or be or become a member of any political club or association or any club or association] intended to affect legislation for on behalf of the street cleaning department or any member thereof.

From section 537 :—

No member of the clerical or uniformed force of the department of street cleaning shall be removed until he has been informed of the cause of the proposed removal and has been allowed an opportunity of making an explanation and in every case of removal the true grounds thereof shall be entered upon the records of the department. * * * * * In the event of the removal of any member of the clerical or uniformed force, he shall have the right to sue out a writ of certiorari or other appropriate remedy for the purposes of reviewing the action of the commissioner or his deputy, and, upon being successful upon such proceeding, he shall be entitled to be reinstated and to receive full pay during the time of his suspension or removal from office.

From article 541 :—

The said commissioner of street cleaning shall have power, and it shall be his duty, to purchase or hire from time to time for his use as such commissioner, at current prices, such and so many horses, carts, steam tugs, scows, boats, vessels, machines, tools and other property as may be required for the economical and effectual performance of his aforesaid duty or to contract for the construction of any such tugs, scows, boats, vessels, carts, machines, tools or other property; or for the sweeping of streets and the removal of street sweepings [by machine,] * * * Provided, that nothing herein contained shall prevent said commissioner, whenever it shall be necessary, to hire such horses, carts, boats, steam tugs, scows, vessels, machines, or tools for a day or trip, and for successive days or trips, without advertising of contract founded on sealed proposals or bids.

From section 544 :—

The terms and conditions of all contracts for street sweeping and cleaning, or for the collection of ashes and garbage, shall, before they are entered into, be approved by the board of estimate and apportionment.

From section 666 :—

The commissioner may appear either by clerk or by counsel on all hearings [and] or proceedings for the commitment of children.

From section 689 relating to appeals in abandonment proceedings:—

If a new trial is ordered it must be had in the court where the appeal was heard, before a judge without a jury.

An appeal to the court of general sessions may be taken in an abandonment proceeding, by the commissioner of public charities in whose name the proceeding is brought, from a decision or judgment of a city magistrate under this chapter, within the county of New York, or to the county court in any other county which is wholly or partly within The City of New York, as constituted by this act.

For the purpose of appealing the commissioner must within sixty days after such decision or judgment make an affidavit showing the alleged errors in the proceeding in which the decision or judgment was rendered, and must within that time present it to the county judge of the county where the proceeding was brought or to a justice of the supreme court in that department, or in the county of New York to the recorder or a judge authorized to hold a court of general sessions, and apply thereon for an allowance of the appeal.

If, in the opinion of the justice, judge or recorder to whom the affidavit is submitted, it is proper that the questions set forth in the affidavit should be decided by the appellate court, he must endorse upon the affidavit an allowance of an appeal to that court. And the commissioner must within five days thereafter serve a copy of such affidavit upon which the appeal was granted, together with a notice that the same has been allowed, upon the defendant in the abandonment proceeding or upon the attorney or counsel who last appeared for the defendant therein.

Sections seven hundred and fifty-five, seven hundred and fifty-six seven hundred and fifty-seven and seven hundred and fifty-eight of the code of criminal procedure shall apply to the appeal herein provided.

The appeal may be brought to argument by the commissioner or the defendant upon ten days' notice to the opposite party, to be served personally on the commissioner or, either personally upon the defendant or personally upon the attorney who last appeared for the defendant.

The appeal shall be heard and disposed of in the manner provided by sections seven hundred and sixty-three, seven hundred and sixty-four, seven hundred and sixty-five, seven hundred and sixty-six and seven hundred and sixty-nine of the code of criminal procedure, except that if a new trial be ordered, it shall be had in the court where the appeal was heard, before a judge without a jury, and, pending such new trial, the judge shall issue a warrant for the arrest of the defendant, and may hold him to bail as upon an indictment.

Upon an appeal taken by the commissioner of public charities no costs shall be awarded to either party.

From section 692:

§ 692. 1. On the first day of [July, nineteen hundred and one] February, nineteen hundred and two, the jurisdiction of the department of public charities of The City of New York over Bellevue Hospital and the Fordham, Harlem and Gouverneur Hospitals and the Emergency Hospital in East Twenty-sixth street in The City of New York, shall cease, and the care, management and control of such hospitals shall be vested in a board of trustees, which shall on said date succeed to all rights, duties and powers heretofore vested in said department of public charities so far as concerns said hospitals. Said board of trustees shall consist of seven residents of The City of New York, together with the [president of the board of public charities until January first, nineteen hundred and two, and thereafter the] commissioner of public charities, ex-officio. * * * [On or before the first day of June.] In the month of January and on or before the twentieth day thereof, prior to the expiration of the term of office of any trustee, the mayor shall appoint his successor for the full term of seven years. * * * Notice in writing of the dates on which appointments, including the first, to said board of trustees are proprosed to be made shall be given by the mayor to each of said presidents or other executive heads at least [five] ten days prior thereto. * * * To enable said commissioners to prepare such plan, they shall have access to all of the books and papers which are the property of The City of New York in the custody of said department of public charities, and to visit said hospitals, and to require at any and all times the attendance before them of the commissioner[s] of public charities and of any of [their] his employees and subordinates.

* * * * * *

It shall be the duty of the board of trustees thereof to send to the board of estimate and apportionment, on or before the first day of September in each year, an estimate in writing of the sum needed for the ensuing year in the same manner and general form as the heads of departments and other boards of the City of New York are required to furnish.

10. Whenever any sick person in Bellevue or other hospitals hereinbefore mentioned shall, in the judgment of the board of trustees, cease to be a proper case for treatment therein, said board may cause such person to be transferred to the care, custody and control of the commissioner of public charities, who shall forthwith receive and care for such person. In case any sick person under treatment in any of said hospitals shall die while under the care of the board of trustees, the latter, by their properly designated officer or employe, may call upon the commissioner of public charities forthwith to receive and remove the body of such person, and it

shall thereupon be the duty of such commissioner forthwith to receive and remove the same for burial or other proper disposition. The cost and expense of such reception, removal, burial or other proper disposition shall be borne and paid by the department of public charities.

[Note:—Other changes are made in section 692 to make its provisions agree with the changes in date above noted.]

From section 694, relating to the commissioner of correction:

His salary shall be [six] seven thousand five hundred dollars a year.

Reports by superintendent of the workhouse, warden and sheriffs.

§ 708. It shall be the duty of the superintendent of the workhouse. [Where a commitment has been made to the workhouse, penitentiary, or county jail, under any of the provisions of section seven hundred and seven of this act, except subdivision two thereof, it shall be the duty of the superintendent, warden, sheriff, or other person having charge of such institution,] to ascertain from the records thereof [of the institution under his charge,] and from examination and inspection of the person committed as aforesaid whether such person has since April fourth, eighteen hundred and ninety-five [January first, nineteen hundred and two,] and within two years next preceding the date of his commitment, been previously committed to such institution upon conviction of public intoxication, disorderly conduct or vagrancy. Within twenty-four hours after the commitment of any such person to the workhouse, [penitentiary or county jail,] the said superintendent, [warden or, sheriff, as the case may be, shall make an examination and take the measurements of any such person according to the system known as the Bertillon system, and] shall transmit to the commissioner a written statement, [certificate] showing the name, [aliases,] sex, age, residence, occupation, height, weight and the color of the hair of any such person, and describing any [the measurements,] scars, marks, or deformities, or other signs whereby such person may subsequently be identified, the date of the commitment, the offense for which such person was committed, and the name of the [court or] magistrate by [which or] whom the such commitment was made. Such statement [certificate] shall also show whether such person has been previously committed to such institution within the period, and for any one of the cause above specified, and, if so, the number of times that such person has been so committed during that period, the date of the last previous commitment of such person for either of said offenses, the name of the [court or] magistrate by [which or by] whom and the offense for which such last previous commitment was made, and the period of detention under such last previous commitment.

From section 720 :—

[The fire commissioner shall have power to appoint and at pleasure remove two deputy commissioners, to be known as first deputy and second deputy. The first deputy shall during the absence or disability of the commissioner possess all the powers and perform all the duties of the commissioner, except the power of making appointments. In the absence or disability of both the commissioner and the first deputy commissioner, the second deputy shall possess and perform all the duties of the commissioner, except the power of making appointments. The commissioner shall define the duties of the deputies, and may delegate to either of them any of his powers except the power of making appointments. The salary of each of such deputies shall be four thousand dollars a year.]

Office in the borough of Brooklyn.

§ 721. The fire commissioner shall appoint a deputy commissioner, who shall be seated at the office of the fire department in the borough of Brooklyn, through whom such business, duties and powers of the fire department in the boroughs of Brooklyn and Queens shall be conducted, performed and exercised, as may be directed by the fire commissioner. The deputy commissioner shall, during the absence or disability of the commissioner, possess all the powers and perform all the duties of the commissioner, throughout the city, except the power of making appointments.

Treasurer.

§723. The fire commissioner shall be the treasurer of the fire department, and shall file in the office of the comptroller a bond in the sum of [one hundred] twenty thousand dollars for the faithful performance of his duties as such treasurer.

From section 733:—

The fire commissioner shall select the grade of cloth and quality required for said uniforms, but shall not prescribe where or of whom said uniforms or uniform clothing shall be purchased, or the price to be paid therefor, and [N] no contractor or agent or employe of any contractor for the making of uniforms for the fire department shall have an office within any building belonging to or under the control of said fire department.

From section 739:—

[Neither the fire commissioner nor any deputy fire commissioner nor any.] No member of the uniformed force shall be permitted to contribute any moneys directly or indirectly to any political fund, or to join or become or be a member of any political club or association, or of any club or association intended to affect legislation for or on behalf of the fire department or any officer or member thereof, or to contribute any money directly or indirectly for such purpose.

Fireworks and explosive compounds; manufacture and sale thereof.

§764. No fireworks, detonating works, cartridges, powder train, percussion caps, collodion, nitrate of soda, nitrate of silver, ether, phosphorus, matches, or explosive compounds, or explosive substances shall hereafter be manufactured [stored, or kept on sale] in the city, except at such places, in such manner, and in such quantities as shall be determined by the said commissioner in the exercise of his discretion, under a permit by him granted therefor, and subject to be revoked at any time by said commissioner. [No quantity of the following-named chemicals, acids and combustible materials greater than is hereinafter enumerated, shall be stored or kept in or upon any one building within the city, namely: sulphur, one thousand pouuds; manufactured matches, five hundred pounds; saltpetre, nitrate of soda, five hundred pounds in the whole; nitrate of silver, collodion, ether, phosphorous, fifty pounds in the whole; aquafortis, muriatic acid, nitric acid and sulphuric acid, not exceeding one thousand pounds in the whole; tar, pitch, rosin, turpentine, one hundred barrels in the whole, except the same shall be stored and kept in such building and manner as said commissioner may require, under a special permit by him issued therefor.]

From section 766:—

[But licenses for this purpose may be granted in the boroughs of Queens and Richmond without the payment of the license fee in this section provided.]

Storage of certain chemicals regulated.

§769. [Except upon the approval of the commissioner.] No quantity of the following-named chemicals and combustible materials greater than is hereafter enumerated shall be stored or kept in, or upon any one building within the city, namely: hemp or flax, unbaled, two thousand pounds in the whole; varnish, [rosin,] twenty barrels in the whole; alcohol, pure spirits, camphene, burning fluid, five barrels in the whole; unslaked lime, ten barrels; vitriol, five carboys in the whole; loose wood shavings, one hundred pounds; [except the same shall be stored and kept upon an open space of ground, surrounded by a wall constructed entirely of fireproof materials, at least twelve feet high and twelve inches thick; or within a fireproof building remote or distant at least fifty feet from any adjacent building,] sulphur one thousand pounds; manufactured matches, five hundred pounds; chlorate of potash, chlorate of soda and other chlorates, saltpetre, nitrate of soda, and other nitrates, five hundred pounds in the whole; collodion, ether, phosphorous, fifty pounds in the whole; cartridges, percussion caps, powder train, sodium peroxide, one hundred pounds in the whole; aquafortis, muriatic acid nitrate acid, not exceeding one thousand pounds in the whole; tar, pitch, rosin and turpentine, one hundred barrels in the whole, except at such places in such manner, and in such quantities as shall be determined by the fire commissioner, in the exercise of his discretion, under a permit by him granted therefor; zinc dust, calcium carbide and metallic sodium shall be limited to one hundred pounds in the whole, and shall not be stored or kept in localities below the grade floor of any building. The commissioner shall prepare or cause to be prepared a list which shall specifically name other chemicals and other compounds or substances, not elsewhere in this section named and limited, which he may ascertain to be liable to ignite or to give off inflammable gases or to generate excessive heat when in contact with water or moisture. Such list of chemicals, compounds and substances shall be added to from time to time and designated and classed in the regulations published by the commissioner as "compounds and substances made dangerous by contact with water or moisture," and such chemicals and other compounds and substances so specifically designated and classed in such regulations shall not be stored or kept in localities below the grade floor of any building, provided, however, that in determining the quantities of said materials and other substances for the storage or keeping of which within the city an application for a permit shall be made, full consideration shall be given to the character of such materials and substances and to the conditions existing in and about the place or building mentioned in the application, and provided that none of the above mentioned articles shall be stored or kept on sale or for business purposes in any building occupied in whole or in part as a dwelling unless by special permit from the commissioner, which permit shall state the quantity that can be so stored or kept in such building. If any decision of the fire commissioner shall be deemed to work an injury to the applicant or to the public, or shall involve a menace to the public safety, the final decision on such application for permit, upon the request of either the fire commissioner or of the applicant for a permit, or the owner of or a tenant in the building where the goods are stored or proposed to be stored, or of a tenant in an adjoining building or of the owner of an adjoining building, shall be referred to a committee of official arbitrators consisting of the fire commissioner or his representative, the president of the New York Board of Trade and Transportation, or his representative, and the chairman of the New York section of the American Chemical society, or his representative, and the decision of such arbitrators shall be binding upon all parties interested in an application for a permit and upon all owners and tenants of any building, the owner or any tenant whereof shall have made application for arbitration as herein provided. The majority vote of said arbitrators shall be necessary to the determination of any issue referred to them. The commissioner shall prepare and publish such regulations as in his judgment may be necessary to control the storage and handling of the materials specified in this section, and he shall from time to time add to such list and bring under such regulations such other materials as the public safety may require. He shall give public notice of such additions by publication of the same in the City Record and by circular notice to such dealers and warehouse men as the records of his department may show to have been granted a permit to handle or store such class or character of goods.

From section 779:—

Said fire marshals shall be members of the uniformed force of the fire department of The City of New York, and within such boroughs, respectively, to which they may be assigned, shall have and possess all the powers heretofore conferred by law upon the fire marshal of the corporation heretofore known as the mayor, aldermen and commonalty of the city of New York.

From section 789:—

The New York fire department relief fund shall consist of:

* * * * * * *

4. All proceeds of suits for penalties, under title three of this chapter, and all license fees payable under the same which may be paid in from or collected in the boroughs of Manhattan, Brooklyn and Bronx, and forty-five per centum of such proceeds of suits for penalties and license fees as may be paid in from or collected in the boroughs of Queens and Richmond. * * * * * * * *

7. Ten per centum annually of all excise moneys or license fees belonging to The City of New York, as constituted by this act, and derived or received by any commissioner of excise or public officer, from the granting of licenses, or permission to sell strong or spirituous liquors, ale, wine or beer, or of any moneys paid for taxes upon the business of trafficking in or selling or dealing in strong or spirituous liquors, ale, wine or beer in the boroughs of Manhattan, Brooklyn, and The Bronx [The City of New York] under the provisions of any law of this state authorizing the granting of any such license or permission; and four and one-half per centum annually of such excise moneys or license fees which are likewise derived or received for the granting of licenses or permission to sell strong or spirituous liquors, ale, wine or beer in the boroughs of Queens and Richmond; the said ten per centum and the said four and one-half per centum thereof to be paid by the comptroller of said city, authorized and required to pay the same to the treasurer of the said relief fund, for the benefit thereof, without any action or authority of or from the board of estimate and apportionment, such sum to amount in each and every year to not more than one hundred and fifty thousand dollars, nor to exceed such an amount, if any, as may be required at the end of any fiscal year to bring the surplus in such relief fund over and above all charges then existing against the same up to the sum of two hundred thousand dollars.

* * * * The treasurer of said fund shall give a bond, with one or more sureties, in the sum of [twenty] one hundred thousand dollars, for the faithful performance of his duties. * * * *

9. There shall be paid to the treasurers of the exempt or veteran volunteer firemen's associations existing in the borough of Queens on the first day of January, nineteen hundred and one, quarterly, by the comptroller of the city of New York, for the benefit of said associations and without

any action or authority of or from the board of estimate and apportionment.

a. Forty-five per centum annually of all proceeds of suits for penalties under title three of this chapter, which may be collected or paid in from the borough of Queens, and of all licensed fees payable under the same which may be collected or paid in from the borough of Queens.

b. Four and one-half per centum annually of all excise moneys or license fees belonging to The City of New York, as constituted by this act, and derived or received by any commissioner of excise or public officer from the granting of licenses or permission to sell strong or spirituous liquors, ale, wine or beer, in the borough of Queens, under the provisions of any law of this state, authorizing the granting of any such licenses or permission.

Said moneys shall be apportioned by said comptroller among all such exempt or veteran volunteer firemen's associations, in proportion to the actual bona fide membership of each such association on the first day of January next preceding the time when such apportionment is made. In determining the membership of such associations, only exempt or honorably discharged volunteer firemen shall be considered as members.

10. There shall be paid to the treasurers of the exempt or veteran volunteer firemen's associations existing in the borough of Richmond on the first day of January, nineteen hundred and one, quarterly, by the comptroller of The City of New York for the benefit of said associations and without any action or authority of or from the board of estimate and apportionment.

a. Forty-five per centum annually of all proceeds of suits for penalties under title three of this chapter, which may be collected or paid in from the borough of Richmond, and of all license fees payable under the same which may be collected or paid in from the borough of Richmond.

b. Four and one-half per centum annually of all excise moneys or license fees belonging to The City of New York, as constituted by this act, and derived or received by any commissioner of excise or public officer from the granting of license or permission to sell strong or spirituous liquors, ale, wine or beer in the borough of Richmond, under the provisions of any law of this state, authorizing the granting of any such licenses or permission.

Said moneys shall be apportioned by said comptroller among all such exempt or veteran volunteer firemen's associations in proportion to the actual bona fide membership of each such association on the first day of January next preceding the time when such apportionment is made. In determining the membership of such associations, only exempt or honorably discharged firemen shall be considered as members.

11. There shall be paid to the treasurer of the firemen's association of the state of New York, who shall pay over the same to the treasurer of the volunteer firemen's home association at Hudson, New York, quarterly, by the comptroller of The City of New York without any action or authority of or from the board of estimate and apportionment.

a. Ten per centum annually of all proceeds of suits for penalties under title three of this chapter which may be collected or paid in from the boroughs of Queens and Richmond, and of all license fees payable under the same which may be collected or paid to from the boroughs of Queens and Richmond.

b. One per centum annually of all excise moneys or license fees belonging to The City of New York, as constituted by this act, and derived or received by any commissioner of excise or public officer from the granting of licenses or permission to sell strong or spirituous liquors, ale, wine or beer in the boroughs of Queens and Richmond, under the provisions of any law of this state, authorizing the granting of any such licenses or permission.

From section 792:—

There shall be deducted from the monthly pay of each officer and fireman of said department, and from the monthly pension of retired members of said department, and from the pay of such other employes of said department as shall heretofore have availed themselves of this provision until, as hereinafter provided, the amount of said fund shall equal the sum of ten thousand dollars, the monthly sum of one dollar, which shall be received and deposited by the treasurer of the relief fund to the credit of the New York fire department life insurance fund. * * * * When the amount of such fund shall equal the sum of [twenty-five] ten thousand dollars, assessment shall only be made to maintain said fund at the said sum of [twenty-five] ten thousand dollars

§ 812*. There shall be paid to the corporation known as the Westchester Exempt Firemen's association of The City of New York, by the foreign fire insurance companies and their agents, doing business in that part of the twenty-fourth ward of the borough of The Bronx, annexed to The City of New York by chapter nine hundred and thirty-four of the laws of eighteen hundred and ninety-five, until the seventeenth day of January in the year nineteen hundred and seventeen, the tax of two per centum upon the receipts for prémiums of such foreign fire insurance companies upon the insurance business done by them in said part of the twenty-fourth ward of the borough of The Bronx, and said Westchester Exempt Firemen's association of The City of New York shall cause the moneys so paid to it to be paid over and disposed of as follows:

* Section has no heading in the bill.

1. To the fire commissioner, for the New York fire department relief fund, forty-five per centum.

2. To the Firemen's association of the state of New York, for the Volunteer Firemen's home at Hudson, New York, ten per centum.

3. The remaining forty-five per centum of said moneys shall be retained by the said Westchester Exempt Firemen's association of The City of New York to its own use.

The said Westchester Exempt Firemen's association of The City of New York shall quarterly in each year render to the fire commissioner and to the Firemen's association of the state of New York a sworn statement in detail of the moneys so collected and paid over by said corporation as aforesaid, and from whom and from what source, on account of said tax during the preceding quarter.

From section 816.

[Board] Commissioner of docks, [commissioners,] appointment, [term of office, president and salaries] and salary.

The head of the department of docks and ferries shall be called the [board] commissioner of docks. [The board of docks shall consist of three persons, to be known as commissioners of docks. They] He shall be a resident [s] of The City of New York, and shall be appointed by the mayor, [and hold their respective offices as provided in chapter four of this act. Said commissioners shall elect one of their number president of said board.] The salary of the said commissioner [president] shall be six thousand dollars a year, [and the salary of each of the other two commissioners shall be five thousand dollars a year.]

§816a. No contracts, agreements, deeds, conveyances, leases or other instruments shall be made or executed by the commissioner of docks, and no rules, regulations or ordinances shall be made by said commissioner, unless the same shall have been first approved by resolution in writing passed by the board of estimate and apportionment. This provision shall not apply to contracts for repairs under the sum of one thousand dollars provided for in section eight hundred and twenty-one of this act.

In sections 817, 818, 819, 820, 821, 822, 824, 825, 826, 827, 828, 829, 830, 831, 832, 834, 836, 837, 838, 844, 846, 847, 848, 849, 850, 851, 852, 853, 854, 856, 857, 858, 860, 865, 866, 867, 869, many verbal changes are made, for the purposes of conforming the language to the substitution of a single commissioner for a board.

From section 821 :—

Provided, however, that repairs not to exceed one thousand dollars in amount on any one dock, pier or bulkhead, may be done by day's work, and without contract, whenever in the judgment of the commissioner [board] of docks it is expedient so to do, and the consent of the board of estimate and apportionment shall have been first obtained.

From section 823 :—

In all proceedings taken prior to the first day of April, nineteen hundred and one, by the board of docks of the City of New York for the acquirement of wharf property, rights, terms, easements or privileges, or lands under water and uplands in The City of New York, if said wharf property or lands under water, or wharf property to which said rights, terms, easements, or privileges are appurtenant, is or are, situated between the southerly side of Bethune street and the northerly side of Gansevoort street, upon or adjacent to the North river in the City of

New York, or between the southerly side of East Eighteenth street and the southerly side of East Twenty-first street, upon or adjacent to the East river, it shall not be necessary for the said board of docks to make any attempt to agree with the owners of any such property, rights, terms, easements, privileges, uplands or lands under water, upon a price for the same, before commencing the proceedings authorized by section eight hundred and twenty-two of this act.

From section 973:—

Upon such an application it shall be lawful for the said court to appoint three discreet and disinterested persons, being citizens of the United States, all of whom shall be residents [and freeholders] of the borough where the property to be taken is located, commissioners of estimate and assessment in said proceeding, for the performance of the duties in this chapter mentioned. * * * * * * * * Ten days' notice of the appointment of the commissioners, Sundays and holidays excluded, shall be published in the City Record and the corporation newspapers, and the corporation counsel shall cause such notice to be served by mail or otherwise upon such parties or their attorneys as have filed a notice of claim or of appearance in the proceeding. The said notice shall specify the names of the persons appointed as commissioners and appoint a day when the parties may be heard at a special term of the supreme court as to the qualifications of the said commissioners. The persons named as commissioners shall attend at the time and place appointed and may be examined under oath as to their qualifications to act. Any ground of challenge which would disqualify a judge or juror shall be applicable to them, and any challenge must be tried and determined by the court in the mode prescribed by law in respect to the challenge of jurors, and such determination may be excepted to and reviewed as in the case of jurors. Where a challenge is sustained and a new commissioner is appointed, such new commissioner shall be subject to challenge in the same way, to be heard and determined by the court at such time as the court may direct.

From section 975 :—

In case of the death, resignation, refusal to act, or failure to qualify within ten days after his appointment of any such commissioner of estimate and assessment, to be appointed under and by virtue of this title, for any such aforesaid purpose, it shall and may be lawful for the court aforesaid, or of any of the justices thereof, on the application of the city, on notice only to any person interested who may have appeared on the prior application, as often as such event shall happen, to appoint a discreet and disinterested person, being a citizen of the United States, and a resident of the borough where the property to be taken is located, in the place and stead of such commissioner so dying, resigning, refusing to act, or failing to qualify. Such successor appointed as aforesaid shall possess the same qualifications and be subject to challenge upon the same grounds and in the same general manner as hereinbefore provided for, and the time and place for such challenge shall be specified in the order appointing such successor.

From section 991, relating to commissioners of estimate and assessment.

The commissioners appointed in pursuance of this title shall complete said proceedings on their part within six months from the time of their appointment, unless further time be allowed by the supreme court. Under penalty of forfeiting all fees to which they would be entitled, unless an extension of time be given to them by the supreme court, which extension shall only be granted in the discretion of the court, upon a written petition containing a full statement by such commissioners, of the reasons necessary for such an extension, and upon notice to the corporation counsel, and to the parties, and their attorneys who have appeared in said proceeding.

From section 999, relating to street opening proceedings.

It shall be the duty of the corporation counsel to present to the justice or referee upon such taxation his certificate in writing that the items of costs, charges and expenses have been audited and examined by him, and also setting forth the result of such audit and examination.

From section 1000, relating to street opening proceedings:—

But in the case of such discontinuance the reasonable actual cash disbursements necessarily incurred and made in good faith by any party interested shall be paid by The City of New York after the same shall have been taxed by a justice of the supreme court, or by a referee under his special order, upon ten days' notice of such taxation being previously given to the corporation counsel.

From section 1002:—

Whenever the owners and proprietors of any such lands, tenements, hereditaments and premises so to be taken for any of the purposes aforesaid or the party or parties, person or persons interested therein, or any, or either of them, the said owners, proprietors, parties or persons in whose favor any such sum or sums, or compensation shall be so reported, shall be under the age of twenty-one years, non compos mentis, [femme covert] or absent from The City of New York, and also in all cases where the name or names of the owner or owners, parties or persons entitled unto or interested in any lands, tenements, hereditaments, or premises that may be so taken for any of the purposes aforesaid, shall not be set forth or mentioned in the said report, or where the said owners, parties, or persons, respectively, being named therein, can not upon diligent inquiry be found, it shall be the duty of [lawful for] the city to pay the sum or sums mentioned in the said report, payable, or that would be coming to such owners, proprietors, parties, and persons, respectively, into the said supreme court, to be secured, disposed of, and invested as the said court shall direct, and such payment shall be as valid and effectual, in all respects, as if made to the said owners, proprietors, parties, and persons, respectively, themselves, according to their just rights, as if they had been known and had all been present, of full age, discovet, and compos mentis; and in default of such payment the said city of New York shall be and remain liable for the amount of the said sums of money with lawful interest thereon from a day one year after the date upon which title vested in The City of New York to the person or persons who may thereafter be found entitled to the same.

From section 1058:—

The powers, duties and functions of all the school boards in the several boroughs within The City of New York, as they have heretofore been constituted, shall cease and determine, and their offices shall be abolished, on the first Monday of February, nineteen hundred and two, and the board of education, as constituted by this act, shall thereupon succeed to such powers, and become subject to such functions and duties as provided by this act.

From section 1059:—

[but nothing contained in this act shall be construed to limit or restrict the power of the board of estimate and apportionment and the municipal assembly to fix in their discretion, and in such detail as they may deem expedient, the amounts to be allowed to said board of education in the annual tax levy.]

[Powers, etc., of school boards, as heretofore constituted, to cease; board of education and the local school boards to succeed to their powers.

§1060. The powers, duties and functions of all the school boards in the several boroughs within the City of New York as they have heretofore been constituted shall cease and determine and their offices shall be abolished on the first Monday of February, nineteen hundred and two, and the board of education, as constituted by this act, shall thereupon succeed to such powers, and become subject to such functions and duties as provided by this act.]

Special and general school fnnds; all moneys to be received administered by board of education.

§ 1060. All moneys raised for educational purposes in The City of New York shall be raised in two funds, to be known as the special school fund, and the general school fund, respectively. The general school fund shall consist of all moneys raised for the payment of salaries of the city superintendent, associate city superintendents and district superintendents, members of the board of examiners, attendance officers, lecturers and all members of the supervising and teaching staff, throughout all boroughs, in conformity with section ten hundred and ninety-one of this act. The special school fund shall contain and embrace all moneys raised for educational purposes not comprised in the general school fund. It shall be the duty of the board of estimate and apportionment and of the board of aldermen to indicate in the budget in raising the special school fund the respective amounts thereof which shall be available for use in the several boroughs. The general school fund shall be raised in bulk, and for the city at large. The board of education shall have power to administer and shall administer all moneys appropriated or available for educational purposes in the City of New York.

From section 1064, relating to the board of education:—

On or before the fifteenth of September in each year it shall submit, an estimate in detail of the moneys needed for the entire school system of the city, during the next succeeding calendar year, to the board of estimate and apportionment for its action. The board of estimate and apportionment shall appropriate for the general school fund for the year nineteen hundred and two, and, annually for each year thereafter, an amount equivalent to not less than four mills on every dollar of assessed valuation of the real and personal estate in The City of New York, liable to taxation. In case the amount so appropriated for the general school fund exceeds the expenditures and ascertained liabilities chargeable to such fund during any one year, the amount by which the said general school fund exceeds said expenditures and liabilities shall become part of the general school fund for the next succeeding year, and the amount to be raised by tax for said fund shall be diminished by the amount of said excess. The board of education shall administer all moneys appropriated or available for educational purposes in The City of New York, subject to the general provisions of this act relating to the audit and payment of salaries and other claims by the department of finance.

From section 1067:—

[The board of education of The City of New York] It shall provide a meeting-room, and such other headquarters, offices and rooms, as [they] it may deem advisable within the boroughs of The City of New York, for the administration of the powers and duties conferred by this chapter upon the board of education, the board of superintendents, and the city superintendent. * * * * * * * * * * * The said board of education shall have power to appoint * * * a supervisor of lectures for the term of six years. * * * The city superintendent of schools, any associate city superintendent, any district superintendent, the supervisor of lectures, any member of the board of examiners, the secretary of the board of education the superintendent of school buildings the superintendent of school supplies, the auditor or auditors and any other officers, clerks or subordinates of the board, may, any or either of them, be removed for cause at any time by a vote of three-fourths of all the members of the board of education, and may be suspended by the board of education pending the trial of charges. The said board shall fix and regulate within the proper appropriation the salaries or compensation of the city superintendent of schools, of the associate city superintendents and the district superintendents, and of members of the board of examiners.

From section 1069:—

The board of education shall, in addition to the other powers herein expressly conferred, have power: * * * * * *

1. To establish and conduct elementary schools, kindergartens, manual training schools, trade schools, truant schools, evening schools and vacation schools, [and schools for colored pupils].

2. To maintain free lectures [within the various buildings under the control of the department of education] and courses of instruction for the people of The City of New York. * * * * *

4. To provide one or more high schools and training schools or classes for teachers, as it may from time to time determine, and as the appropriations may permit. The said training schools or classes shall be under the control of the board of education and of the city superintendent of schools to the extent that may be necessary to secure compliance with chapter one thousand and thirty-one of the laws of eighteen hundred and ninety-five.

From 1078, relating to the city superintendent of schools:—

He shall enforce the compulsory education law, and shall nominate attendance officers to the board of education, and shall direct such officers in their duties. * * * Twenty-three of [t] The district superintendents shall be assigned by the city superintendent to the work of supervision in the local school board districts, to be constituted as hereinafter provided, in such manner that [each] one district superintendent shall be assigned to such duty in [three] two of such districts for the period of one [half the] school year, [and one of such superintendents shall be assigned to a fourth district in addition]. * * * District superintendents, when not so assigned to such duty in said districts, shall be assigned by the city superintendent to such other professional duties as the welfare of the school system may require.

From section 1079:—

There shall be [six] eight associate city superintendents, who, with the city superintendent, shall constitute the board of superintendents. They shall be appointed by the board of education by a vote of a majority of its members, and shall serve for the term of six years, provided, however, * * * and provided also that the other [two] four associate city superintendents shall be appointed from the associate borough superintendents in office on the first day of January, nineteen hundred and two. * * * * * There shall be [fifteen] twenty-six district superintendents to be appointed by the board of education for the term of six years upon the nomination of the board of superintendents, provided, however, that [such district superintendents shall be selected in the first instance from] the associate borough superintendents in office on the first day of January, nineteen hundred and two, [and, when so selected, they] shall serve out as associate city superintendents or as district superintendents the terms for which they were appointed as such borough superintendents by the respective borough school boards heretofore existing. * * * [Any associate city superintendent or any district superintendent may be removed for cause at any time by a two-thirds vote of all the members of the board of education.] * * * * [A r] Resignations of the city superintendent and the associate city superintendents shall be made to the board of education. [Resignations of the associate city superintendents shall be made to the board of education.] Resignations of the district superintendents and directors of special branches shall be made to the board of superintendents. * * * * No person shall be eligible for election as director of a special branch, such as music, drawing, kindergarten, etc., who is not: (a) A graduate of a [high school or of an institution of equal or higher scholastic rank,] college or university recognized by the University of the State of New York; and (b) a graduate from a course of professional training of at least [one] two years in the special branch that he is to supervise or teach; and (c) a teacher of that special branch with at least three years of successful experience. Nothing in this act contained shall prevent the re-election of any superintendent in office at the time of the passage of this act.

From section 1080:—

Under the supervision and direction of the city superintendent, district superintendents shall visit every school in the district to which they are assigned, [respectively, as above provided].

From section 1085, relating to teachers of special branches:—

[Such teachers shall be responsible to the principal of such school wherein they are assigned and to the district superintendent for the performance of their duties therein.]

From section 1086:—

Subject to regulations prescribed by the board of superintendents and under the supervision of the district superintendent in charge, the principal of each school shall direct the methods of teaching in all classes under his charge.

From section 1089:—

The city superintendent of schools shall have power with the consent of the board of education to employ assistants temporarily at rates to be fixed by the board of education, [or to assign one or more of the district superintendents, to aid said board of examiners]. * * * * * No associate city superintendent, district superintendent, principal or teacher in The City of New York shall be allowed to serve on the board of examiners, [except as herein otherwise provided]. * * *

* All pupils who entered the Normal College in The City of New York on or before February first, eighteen hundred and ninety-eight, shall upon graduation therefrom be exempted from further examination under this section, and shall upon such graduation be entitled to licenses to teach as regular teachers in The City of New York.

From section 1090 :—

Teachers and principals may be promoted or transferred from one school to any other school within the city by the board of superintendents subject to the approval of the board of education; provided, however, that a teacher shall not be transferred from a school in one borough to a school in another borough without his or her consent. For all purposes affecting the appointment, promotion or transfer of the teachers in any school, the district superintendent assigned to the district in which such school is situated, the principal of such school and, in the case of transfer, the district superintendent and the principal of the school to which it is proposed to transfer a teacher, shall have seats in the board of superintendents, with votes on such propositions. * * Existing eligible lists in The City of New York and the relative standing of persons whose names are on said lists shall not be affected by the passage of this act.

From section 1091 :—

The board of education shall have power to adopt by-laws fixing [after the first day of January, nineteen hundred and two, the board of aldermen, in the recommendation of the board of estimate and apportionment shall fix] the salaries of all members of the supervising and the teaching staff; and the salaries of all principals and teachers shall be regulated by merit, grade of class taught, length of service, experience in teaching, or by a combination of these considerations. [Said salaries need not be uniform throughout the several boroughs, nor in any two of them, nor throughout any one borough. The salaries fixed and established and duly payable to members of the supervising and teaching staff on the thirty-first day of December, eighteen hundred and ninety-nine, shall be and remain after the first day of July, nineteen hundred and one, the salaries of said supervising and teaching staff, unless on or before the said first day of July, nineteen hundred and one, the then existing board of estimate and apportionment shall adopt, new schedules of salaries, and said board of estimate and apportionment is expressly empowered to adopt such new schedules. On or before June fifteenth, nineteen hundred and one, the board of education shall submit to the said board of estimate and apportionment such schedules of salaries as in its judgment should be adopted; but nothing herein contained shall be held to limit the discretion of the board of estimate and apportionment in regard thereto. Until the said first day of July, nineteen hundred and one, the salaries now payable by law shall continue to be payable.] Such by-laws shall establish a uniform schedule of salaries for the supervising and the teaching staff throughout all boroughs which schedule shall provide for an equal annual increment of salary of such an amount, that no kindergartner, or female teacher of girls' class other than those teaching grades of the last two years in the elementary schools shall, after sixteen years of service in said schools, receive less than twelve hundred and forty dollars per annum; and no female teacher of a girls' class of the grades of the last two years in said school shall, after fifteen years of service in said schools, receive less than thirteen hundred and twenty dollars per annum; and no female teacher of a girls' graduating class, female first assistant, or female vice-principal, shall after ten years of service in said schools, receive less than fourteen hundred and forty dollars per annum ; and no female teacher of a boys' or a mixed class shall receive less than sixty dollars per annum more than a female teacher of a girls' class of a corresponding grade and of years of service ; and no female teacher in said elementary schools shall receive less than six hundred dollars per annum, nor shall the annual increment for any female teacher therein be less than forty dollars; and no male teacher of a class of the grades of the last two years in said schools, shall, after twelve years of service in said schools, receive less than twenty-one hundred and sixty dollars per annum ; and no male teacher of a graduating class, male first assistant, or male vice-principal shall, after ten years of service in said schools receive less than twenty-four hundred dollars per annum; and no male teacher in said elementary schools shall receive less than nine hundred dollars per annum, nor shall the annual increment for any male teacher therein be less than one hundred and five dollars; that no female head of department, or female assistant to the principal in said schools shall receive less than sixteen hundred dollars per annum after ten years of service; and no male head of department or male assistant to the principal in said schools shall receive less than twenty-four hundred dollars per annum after ten years of service; that in high schools and training schools for teachers, no female junior or substitute teacher, female laboratory or library assistant, or female clerk, shall receive less than seven hundred dollars per annum, nor after six years of service as such, less than one thousand dollars per annum; no female model teacher shall receive less than one thousand dollars per annum; nor after five years of service as such, less than fifteen hundred dollars per annum ; no female regular teacher in said schools shall receive less than eleven hundred dollars per annum, nor after ten years of service as such, less than nineteen hundred dollars per annum , no female head teacher, female assistant to the principal, female first assistant, or female vice-principal in said schools shall receive less than two thousand dollars per annum, nor after five years of service as such, less than twenty-five hundred dollars per annum; no male junior or substitute teacher, male laboratory or library assistant, or male clerk, shall receive less than nine hundred dollars per annum, nor after six years of service as such, less than twelve hundred dollars per annum; no male regular teacher in said schools shall receive less than thirteen hundred dollars per annum, nor after ten years of service as such, less than twenty-four hundred dollars per annum; no male head teacher, male assistant to the principal, male first assistant, or male vice-principal in said schools, shall receive less than twenty-five hundred dollars per annum, nor after five years of service as such, less than three thousand dollars per annum; nor shall any of said persons therein receive a salary less than that to which by reason of experience such person would be entitled as a teacher of the aforesaid elementary schools; provided, however, that none of the aforesaid members of the supervising and the teaching staff of any of the elementary schools shall receive a salary greater than that fixed for the seventh year of service unless and until the service of any such member shall have been approved after inspection and investigation as fit and meritorious by a majority of the board of superintendents, that none of the aforesaid members of the supervising and the teaching staff of any of the elementary schools shall receive a salary greater than that fixed for the twelfth year of service, unless and until the service of any such member shall have been approved after inspection and investigation as fit and meritorious by a majority of the board of superintendents; that none of the aforesaid members of the supervising and the teaching staff of any of the high or training schools shall receive a salary greater than that fixed for the fourth year of the service unless and until the service of any such member shall have been approved after inspection and investigation as fit and meritorious by a majority of the board of superintendents ; and that none of the aforesaid members of the supervising and the teaching staff of any of the high or training schools shall receive a salary greater than that fixed for the ninth year of service unless and until the service of any such member shall have been approved after inspection and investigation as fit and meritorious by a majority of the board of superintendents ; and the board of superintendents shall approve or disapprove the service of the aforesaid members of the supervising and teaching staff within forty days before the date on which said members shall, respectively, become eligible to the increase of salaries conditioned upon the approval of said service. For the purposes affecting such increases of salaries of said persons in any schools, the district superintendent assigned to the district in which such school is situated shall have a seat in the board of superintendents, with a vote on such fitness and merit ; that no female branch principal of an elementary school having not less than twelve classes shall receive less than twenty-five hundred dollars per annum after ten years of service as such in said schools; and no male branch principal or male principal of an elementary or a high school having not less than twelve classes shall receive less than thirty-five hundred dollars per annum after ten years of service as such in said schools; and a principal of said schools shall receive an equal annual increment of two hundred and fifty dollars; provided, however, that the service of such principal or branch principal shall have been approved after inspection and investigation as fit and meritorious by a majority of the board of superintendents; and no principal of a high school or training school for teachers having supervision of not less than twenty-five teachers therein shall receive less than five thousand dollars per annum. The board of examiners shall issue to a principal or a teacher who has had experience in schools other than the schools of The City of New York, a certificate stating that the experience of such teacher is equivalent to a certain number of years of experience in the schools of the said city. The board of examiners shall issue to a principal or teacher who has had experience in schools other than the high and training schools of The City of New York, certificate stating that the experience of such teacher is equivalent to a certain number of years of experience in the high and training schools of the said city. Such certificates made by the board of examiners shall be final and conclusive on all matters pertaining to experience therein stated, and shall entitle their holders to salaries in accordance with the schedules of salaries established in conformity with this section, in like manner as though the years mentioned in such certificates had been served in those schools of The City of New York that are respectively mentioned in such certificates. No salary now paid to any member of the supervising and the teaching staff of any of the public schools in The City of New York shall be reduced by the operation of this section; and the aforesaid equal annual increment for each class or grade of the supervising and the teaching staff of said public schools shall be uniform throughout each class or grade, and each of said persons shall at once receive all the emolument in accordance with the above sehedule of minimum salaries to which said person is entitled by reason of merit, of experience and of grade of class taught.

From section 1092, relating to the public school teachers' retirement fund :—

And the comptroller of The City of New York shall report in detail to the board of education of The City of New York, annually, in the month of January, the condition of said fund, and the items of the receipts and disbursements on account of the same. The said retirement fund shall consist of the following, with the interest and income thereof: * * * * (3) Five per centum annually of all excise moneys or license fees belonging to The City of New York and derived or received by any commisssoner of excise or public officer, from the granting of licenses or permission to sell strong or spirituous liquors, ale, wine or beer in The City of New York, under the provisions of any law of this state authorizing the granting of any such licenses or permission. The comptroller of The City of New York shall hold such moneys, together with any other moneys belonging to said fund, and by direction of the said board of education shall have charge of and administer the same as hereinbefore in this section provided. (4) [Such an amount not exceeding one hundred thousand dollars as may be required to bring the surplus in such fund up to one hundred thousand dollars and as may be provided for in the annual budget by the board of estimate and apportionment and the board of aldermen.] All such other methods of increment as may be duly and legally devised for the increase of said fund. * * * * [Said] On the recommendation of the city superintendent, said board of education shall have power, by a two-thirds vote of all its members [and after recommendation to that effect shall have been made by the city superintendent of schools, stating that the teacher is mentally or physically incapacitated for the performance of duty,] to retire any member of the teaching or supervising staff, including the members of the board of examiners, who is mentally or physically incapacitated for the performance of duty, and has been engaged in the work of teaching or school supervision for [any female teacher of the public schools, including special teachers in the same, who shall have taught therein during] a period aggregating thirty years, twenty of which have been in the public schools of The City of New York, [and to retire any male teacher of said schools who shall have taught therein during a period aggregating thirty-five years.] And the board of education may retire from active service any member of the said teaching or supervising staff who shall have attained the age of sixty-five years and shall have been engaged in the work of teaching or school supervision for a period aggregating thirty years, [in the case of female teachers and thirty-five years in the case of male teachers,] twenty of which shall have been in the public schools of The City of New York. The said board of education shall also have power by a two-thirds vote of all its members, and after a recommendation to that effect shall have been made by the board of trustees of the Normal college stating that the teacher is mentally or physically incapacitated for the performance of duty, to retire the female superintendent and any female tutors of the Normal college and the female superintendent and any female critic teacher of the training department of the Normal college who shall have taught in said Normal college or training department or in the public schools during a period aggregating thirty years. The said board of education upon the recommendation of the trustees of the Normal college may also, in its discretion, retire any such teacher or teachers upon her or their own application after the like period of service. All money, pay, compensation or salary or any part thereof forfeited, deducted or withheld from any female superintendent or superintendents or any female teacher or teachers of the Normal college and training department for and on account of absence from duty for any cause shall be turned into the teachers' retirement fund by the board of trustees of said college. Any teacher. [or] principal or supervising official, including members of the board of examiners, so retired shall thereafter be entitled to receive as an annuity one-half the annual salary paid to said teacher, [or] principal or supervising official at the date of said retirement, not to exceed, however, [in any] case the case of a teacher, the sum of one thousand dollars per annum, in the case of a principal fifteen hundred dollars per annum, and in the case of a supervising official, two thousand dollars per annum. And in no case shall such annuity for any teacher, already retired or hereafter to be retired, be less than six hundred dollars. The said board is hereby given the power to use both the principal and the income of said fund. [Any surplus in the retirement fund over and above one hundred thousand dollars shall be transferred into the general fund for the reduction of taxation.]

From section 1093, relating to charges against teachers:

The board of education, on receiving notice of such charges [under the provisions of either of the foregoing paragraphs], shall immediately proceed to try and determine the case, either in the board or by a committee of its body, and shall fix the [fine] penalty or punishment, if, any, [that should] to be imposed for the offense, and such [fine] penalty or punishment shall consist of a fine, [in] suspension for a fixed time without pay, or [in] dismissal, provided, however, that a vote of a majority of all the members of the board of education shall be necessary to impose the penalty of dismissal.

From section 1095:

The board of education shall, between the first day of August and the thirtieth day of November in each year, make and transmit to the mayor of The City of New York a report in writing, [bearing date on,] for the year ending [with] on the thirty-first day of July preceding. * * The board of education shall also make in [either of] said reports such suggestions and recommendations relative to the public schools of The City of New York as it may deem proper.

From section 1097, relative to books of records to be kept by the board of education:—

These books shall be preserved as the property of the board of education and, [school, and such books] shall at all times be opened to inspection [access] by members of the board of education, by members of the local school boards and by the city superintendent, or by any associate city superintendent, or by the district superintendents.

Contributions to political funds, etc., prohibited.

§ 1099. Neither the city superintendent of schools, nor any associate or district superintendent of schools, nor any member of the board of examiners, nor any member of the supervising or teaching staff of the department of education of The City of New York, shall be permitted to contribute any moneys, directly or indirectly, to any [political fund, or to join or be or become a member of any club or association] fund intended to affect [or engaged in affecting] legislation increasing their emoluments.

From section 1101, relating to employes under the public school system:—

Except as herein otherwise provided, * * * all principals, teachers and other members of the educational staff in the public school system of any part of the City of New York, and all school officers or other employes appointed by the board of education before this act takes effect * * * shall continue to hold their respective positions and to be entitled to such compensation as is now provided or may hereafter be provided by the lawful authority subject to change of title, to reassignment or to removal of cause, as may be provided by law, and subject to the right of the said board to abolish unnecessary positions. The secretaries, clerical force and employes of the several borough school boards abolished by this act, including the supervisor of lectures for the boroughs of Manhattan and the Bronx, shall be assigned by the board of education, and the clerical force and the employes of the several borough superintendents and boards of borough superintendents also abolished by this act shall be assigned by the board of superintendents, to positions and duties corresponding as nearly as may be to their respective positions and duties before this act takes effect without prejudice or advantage. All licenses to teach or certificates of qualifications for teaching granted by the superintendent of public instruction of the city of Brooklyn, or by authority of the board of education of the said city of Brooklyn, prior to February first, eighteen hundred and ninety-eight, or recognized by the board of education of the said city of Brooklyn or the state superintendent of public instruction as in force at that date in said city, shall unless revoked for cause by the state superintendent of public instruction, be recognized by the city superintendent of schools and the board of examiners of The City of New York, as in full force, and shall entitle the holders to appointment or promotion to any position to which they were respectively eligible by the possession of such licenses or certificates.

From section 1152 :—

The school established and maintained by the Five Points House of Industry, in The City of New York, the school established and maintained by the Ladies' Home Missionary Society of the Methodist Episcopal Church, at the institution in Park street, near the place usually called the Five Points, in the said city, and the industrial schools established and maintained under the charge of the Children's Aid Society, in The City of New York, or any other private school in the said city in the discretion of the board of education, shall participate through the board of education in the distribution of the common school fund in the same manner and degree as the common schools in The City of New York, and shall be subject to the same regulations and restrictions as are now by law imposed on the common schools of New York.

CHAPTER XIX.

DEPARTMENT OF HEALTH.

Title 7 [Tenement and] Lodging houses.

From section 1172:—

Said board of health [the board of aldermen] is hereby authorized and empowered, from time to time, to add to and to alter, amend or annul any part of the said sanitary code, and may therein publish additional provisions for the security of life and health in The City of New York, and confer additional powers on the department of health, not inconsistent with the constitution or laws of this state, and may provide for the enforcement of the said sanitary code by such fines, penalties, forfeitures, or imprisonment as made by ordinance be prescribed. The board of [aldermen] health may embrace in said sanitary code all matters and subjects to which, and so far as, the power and authority of said department of health extends.

Publication of reports and statistics.

§ 1175. The board of health may establish as it shall deem wise, and to promote the public good and public service, reasonable regulations as to the publicity of any of the papers, files, reports, records and proceedings of the department of health; and may publish such information as may, in its opinion, be useful, concerning births, deaths, marriages, sickness, and the general sanitary conditions of said city, or any matter, place or thing therein. [Said department shall prepare and keep the statistics of tenements and lodging houses, and make semi-annual reports upon the same, and transmit such statistics to the state board of health.]

From section 1179:—

There shall be two bureaus in the department of health. The chief officer [officers] of one bureau shall be called the "sanitary superintendent[s]" who [and] at the time of his [their respective] appointment[s], shall have been, for at least ten years, a practising physician[s], and for three years a residents of The City of New York, and he shall be the chief executive officer of said departments. The chief officer[s] of the second bureau shall be called the "registrar[s] of records."

From section 1181:—

The board of health shall establish and maintain in the boroughs of Manhattan, [and] The Bronx, Brooklyn, Queens and Richmond, offices wherein the business and duties of the department of health shall be performed and discharged under its rules, regulation and control. To this end [T] the [commissioner] board of health shall appoint [two] assistant sanitary superintendents, and [two] assistant registrars of records, one of each of such officers to be assigned to each of the [two] five borough offices above mentioned, and so many of the other officers, clerks, inspectors and subordinates allowed, pursuant to this chapter, as may be necessary to conduct and transact the business of the health department, in each of the said boroughs, [into which The City of New York is divided by this act]. * * * * The board of health may likewise establish such other additional offices as it shall deem necessary for the proper discharge of the duties and powers of the health department in the several boroughs, with such force as may be essential thereto throughout the city as constituted by this act, but shall always maintain its chief office in the Borough of Manhattan.

From section 1182:—

The board of health and the commissioner of health may from time to time delegate any portion of its or his powers to the sanitary superintendent or an assistant sanitary superintendent, to be exercised by such delegates from the time and in the manner, and to the extent specified in such delegation in writing. * * * * The board of health may designate a clerk to be the chief clerk of the department, and a clerk in each of the offices of the five boroughs above mentioned, in which offices are established, to be an assistant chief clerk, who may perform such duties of the secretary as shall be assigned to him; and papers certified by such chief clerk or by an assistant chief clerk shall be of the same effect as evidence and otherwise as is certified by the secretary.

From section 1183:—

It shall be the duty of the sanitary superintendent and the assistant sanitary superintendents, as each may be directed, to execute, or cause to be executed, the orders of said department of health and generally, according to instructions, to exercise a practical supervision in respect to the inspectors, agents, and persons other than the secretary, and health commissioner, and as to the members of the police force, who may exercise any authority under this chapter.

From section 1184:—

The sanitary superintendent, the assistant sanitary superintendents, the sanitary inspectors and the officers of said department may all visit sick persons, who shall be reported to the department of health as sick of any contagious, pestilential, or infectious disease and report to the department of health, in writing, his or their opinion of their sickness.

From section 1185:—

The [commissioner] board of health shall appoint and commission at least fifty sanitary inspectors, and shall have power to appoint twenty additional sanitary inspectors, if [the board of health] it deems that number necessary, and from time to time to prescribe the duties of each of said inspectors, and the place of their performance, and of all other persons exercising any authority under said department, except as herein specially provided.

From section 1188 :—

The members of the board of health, the health commissioners, the sanitary superintendent, the assistant sanitary superintendents, and any of the sanitary inspectors, and such other officer or person as may, at any time, be, by said board of health authorized, may, without fee or hindrance, enter, examine and survey all grounds, erections, vehicles, structures, apartments, buildings, and every part thereof, and places in the city, including vessels of all kinds in the waters, and all cellars, sewers, passages and excavations of every sort, and inspect the safety and sanitary condition, and make plans, drawings and descriptions thereof, according to the order or regulations of said department.

From section 1189.—

Proofs, affidavits and examinations as to any matter under this chapter may be taken by or before the board of health or other person, as the board of health shall authorize; and the commissioner of health, the secretary, the sanitary superintendent, assistant sanitary superintendents and any member of said department shall, severally, have authority to administer oaths in such matters, and any person guilty of willfully answering or testifying falsely therein shall incur all the pains and penalties of perjury.

Salaries.

§1194. The annual salaries to be paid to persons herein named, and appointed to the several specified positions, shall, from and after their entrance upon their duties, be as follows, and such salaries shall be in full for all services rendered by them to the city in any capacity whatever: To the commissioner of health, seven thousand five hundred dollars; to the sanitary [superintendents each] superintendent, five thousand dollars; to the secretary, five thousand dollars; to the assistant sanitary superintendents, each three thousand five hundred dollars; to the registrar of records, four [each three] thousand dollars; to the assistant registrars of records, each three thousand dollars; to the chief clerk of the department of health, three thousand dollars.

From section 1195:—

[Neither the commissioner of health, nor any sanitary superintendent, nor any sanitary inspector shall be permitted to contribute any moneys directly or indirectly to any political fund or to join or to be or become a member of any political club or association intended to affect legislation for or in behalf of the health department or any member thereof, or to contribute any funds for such purpose.]

Sanitary company of police.

§1202a [1324]. The board of health shall make requisition upon the police commissioner [board] for the detail of [at least fifty and] not more than [one hundred] fifty suitable officers and men of at least five years' service in the police force, who shall be selected for their peculiar fitness, for the enforcement of the provisions of the sanitary code [and the acts relating to tenement and lodging houses.] These officers and men shall be detailed to such service by the police commissioner [board] and the department of health shall pay to the police department monthly, the amount of the pay of the officers and men so detailed, who shall belong to the sanitary company of the police and shall report to the board of health. [At least thirty of the officers and men so detailed shall be employed exclusively in the enforcement of the laws relating to tenement and lodging houses.] The board of health may report back to the police commissioner [board] for punishment, any member of said company guilty of any breach of orders or discipline, or of neglecting his duty, and thereupon the police [board] commissioner shall detail another officer or man in his place, and the discipline of the said members of the sanitary company shall be in the jurisdiction of the police department; but at any time the board of health may object to the efficiency of any member of said sanitary company and thereupon another officer or man shall be detailed in his place.

[NOTE. The original of the above section is section 1324 of the charter, which is printed under the same number and without change in the bill as proposed by the charter revision commission.]

From section 1205:—

The board of health shall have full and exclusive power and authority over the removal of night soil, and in the removal of dead animals, offal, night soil, blood, bones, tainted or impure meats, and other refuse matter from said city. It is hereby charged with the duty of causing the removal of the same daily, from the thickly populated districts, or as often as may be necessary elsewhere, and of keeping the said city clean from all matter of nuisance of a similar kind.

From section 1225.

For the purpose of more effectually preventing the spread of smallpox by the thorough and systematic vaccination of all unvaccinated persons, and for the relief of persons suffering with diphtheria and other infectious diseases residing in said city, the board of health is hereby empowered to continue or organize a corps of vaccinators and of physicians, within and subject to the control of the bureau of sanitary inspection, to appoint the necessary officers, keep suitable records, collect and preserve pure vaccine lymph or virus, and produce diphtheria antitoxine and other antitoxines, and add to the sanitary code such additional provisions as will most effectually secure the end in view.

From section 1226.

The avails of such lymph or virus and diphtheria antitoxine, and other antitoxines, shall be accounted for and paid to the chamberlain, and shall be set apart and constitute distinct funds, to be known respectively as "the fund for gratuitous vaccination," and "the antitoxine fund," and they shall be subject to the requisition of the board of health for the purposas named in the preceding section.

Section 1299 of the bill is the same as section 1315 of the present charter, which appears unchanged under that number in the bill of the Revision Commission.

Section 1300 of the bill is the same as section 1316 of the present charter, which appears unchanged under that number in the bill of the Revision Commission.

Title 7 of chap. XIX. of the charter is entitled "Tenement and lodging houses" (sections 1304—1318 in the bill.) The bill would take out all reference to tenement houses. The commission's bill would not make this change.

[Sanitary company of police.]

[Section 1324. The board of health shall make requisition upon the police board for the detail of at least fifty and not more than one hundred suitable officers and men of at least five years' service in the police force, who shall be selected for their peculiar fitness, for the enforcement of the provisions of the sanitary code and the acts relating to tenement and lodging houses. These officers and men shall be detailed to such service by the police board, and the department of health shall pay to the police department monthly, the amount of the pay of the officers and men so detailed, who shall belong to the sanitary company of the police and shall report to the board of health. At least thirty of the officers and men so detailed shall be employed exclusively in the enforcement of the laws relating to tenement and lodging houses. The board of health may report back to the police board for punishment, any member of said company guilty of any breach of orders or discipline, or of neglecting his duty, and thereupon the police board shall detail another officer or man in his place, and the discipline of the said members of the sanitary company shall be in the jurisdiction of the police department; but at any time the board of health may object to the efficiency of any member of said sanitary company and thereupon another officer or man shall be detailed in his place.]

From section 1320 [1332]:—

[Any surplus in the health department pension found over and above twenty-five thousand dollars shall be transferred to the general fund for the reduction of taxation.]

[Repeal of acts inconsistent with this title.]

[§1339. All acts and parts of acts inconsistent with this title are hereby repealed].

Certificate required in certain cases.

§1323. [1335].—No physician or employe, as aforesaid, of the health department, shall be awarded, granted or paid a pension on account of physical or mental disability or disease, unless upon certificate and report of a board of physicians to be appointed by the board of health, which shall set forth the cause, nature and extent of the disability, disease or injury of such physician or employe, who may be placed on the pension roll, and such certificate shall distinctly state whether or not such disability, disease or injury was incurred or sustained by such physician or employe while in the performance of his duties as such physician or employe of the health department, and such certificate shall, in such case, be filed with, and entered upon the minutes of the board of health.

Pension for twenty years' service.

§1323a. Any physician or employe who has or shall have performed duty as such physician or employe in any department of health in The City of New York, for a period of twenty years, or upward, upon his own application, in writing, or upon a certificate and report of a board of physicians, appointed by the board of health, certifying that such physician or employe is permanently disabled, so as to be unfit for further duty as such physician or employe, shall be retired from active service by resolution of the board of health of the health department of The City of New York, and placed upon the health department pension roll, and thereupon shall be awarded, granted and paid from said health department pension fund by the trustees thereof, an annual sum during his lifetime not exceeding one half the ordinary full pay of a physician or employe in the health department service, of the rank of the physician or employe so retired, provided, however, that no pension granted under this or the preceding sections, shall exceed the sum of twelve hundred dollars per annum. Pensions granted under this section shall be for the natural life of the person receiving the same, and shall not be revoked, repealed or diminished. In determining the term of service of any such physician or employe, under this section, service in former health departments or board of health having jurisdiction in matters of public health in any part of The City of New York, as constituted by this act, shall be counted and held to be service in the department of health of The City of New York.

Order of discontinuance of pension in certain cases.

§1324. [§1337.] The board of health may, in its discretion, order any pension granted or any part thereof to cease, except as provided in the last preceding section, but in all such cases the said board of health, shall file with the board of trustees [trustee] of the health department pension fund, a written statement of the causes determining the action of the said board of health in ordering any pension to so cease; and nothing in this act or in any other act, shall render the granting or payment of such pension obligatory on the board of health, or upon the trustees of the health department pension fund, or chargeable as a matter of right upon said fund, except as provided in the last preceding section.

The bill would introduce a new chapter numbered XIX A, entitled "Tenement House Department." The provisions of this chapter are those proposed by the Tenement House Commission, which reported recently to the legislature. The head of the department would be a tenement house commissioner appointed by the mayor. The Revision Commission's bill does not contain this chapter. The chapter embraces sections 1326-1344 p.

From section 1373 :—

The said justices shall in like manner also appoint the officers necessary to attend the court in each district, not exceeding three, at an annual salary of one thousand dollars, and a stenographer in and for each district at an annual salary of two thousand dollars, and in and for each district in the boroughs of Manhattan and Brooklyn an interpreter at an annual salary of twelve hundred dollars. Each of said attendants, stenographers and interpreters shall be appointed for two years or to fill the residue of an unexpired term. The said justices may remove any of said attendants, [or] stenographers or interpreters, provided that before removal such officers shall have notice of the cause of their proposed removal and an opportunity to make an explanation ; and the reasons for any removal shall be briefly entered on such minutes.

§ 1384. In any and all actions brought in the name of The City of New York, or of any department, board, or officer thereof, by the corporation counsel of The City of New York, as attorney for said city, or said department, board or officer thereof, to recover a penalty or penalties for the violation of any law or ordinance, the summons may be issued out of said court by the corporation counsel in his own name without the same being subscribed by the clerk of the court where such action or actions are brought, and in such actions the corporation counsel shall not be required to pay to the clerk of the court the fees in the action, but shall account therefor to the city treasury and shall collect the same, from the defendant, when judgment is recovered; and no fees or costs shall be demanded of the said The City of New York or any department board or officer thereof in any such suit or proceeding.

Board of magistrates.

§ 1391. In each of said divisions, there shall be a board of city magistrates composed of the city magistrates therein in office on the first day of January, nineteen hundred and two, and such as thereafter may be appointed or elected pursuant to law. The board for the first division shall consist of twelve magistrates, each of whom shall be a resident and elector within said first division. [In filling vacancies occurring in the first division after the first day of January, nineteen hundred and two, the mayor shall appoint two magistrates from the borough of The Bronx, so that the board for the first division shall consist of twelve magistrates, ten of whom shall be residents and electors of the borough of Manhattan and two of the borough of The Bronx.] The board of the second division shall consist of [thirteen] fifteen magistrates, [eight] ten of whom shall be residents and electors of the borough of Brooklyn, three of the borough of Queens and two of the borough of Richmond, which said board shall be created as hereinafter provided.

From Section 1392:—

Upon the happening of any vacancy in said office in the first division, whether by expiration of a term or for any other cause, the mayor shall appoint some proper person to fill such vacancy within thirty days after the same occurs; and in case such vacancy occurs otherwise than by expiration of a term, the person appointed to fill the same shall be appointed for the unexpired residue of the term.

The city magistrates in office in the second division on the first day of January, nineteen hundred and one, who were police justices in the former city of Brooklyn in office on the thirty-first day of January, eighteen hundred and ninety-eight, shall hold office until their successors are elected at the general election to be held in the year nineteen hundred and one, but all city magistrates in the borough of Brooklyn appointed after January thirty-first, eighteen hundred and ninety-nine, who were in office on January first, nineteen hundred and one shall hold office until their successors are elected at the general election to be held in the year nineteen hundred and seven.

The terms of the present city magistrates of the second division of the city of New York, who were formerly police justices in the former city of Brooklyn, shall expire on the thirty-first day of December, nineteen hundred and one, and their successors who shall be elected at the general election to be held in the year nineteen hundred and one shall take office on the first day of January in the year nineteen hundred and two. The successors of such magistrates shall at all times thereafter be elected at the general election to be held in the year at the end of which the term of said city magistrates shall expire, and shall be residents and electors of the borough from which said magistrates who they shall be elected to succeed were appointed or elected, and shall hold office for six years. Upon the happening of any vacancy in said office of city magistrate in the second division, whether by expiration of a term or for any other cause the same shall be filled at the next ensuing general election at which a city magistrate can be elected, for the unexpired term commencing on the first day of January after such election, and the mayor shall appoint some proper person to fill such vacancy in the interim.

At the general election to be held in the borough of Brooklyn in the year nineteen hundred and one, there shall be elected in each congressional district, as then constituted in said borough, one city magistrate, and in the territory constituting the borough of Brooklyn there shall be elected two city magistrates at large, and the terms of office of all said city magistrates so elected shall commence on the first day of January nineteen hundred and two and continue for six years thereafter. The successors of said city magistrates in the borough of Brooklyn shall be elected for the like term and in the like manner at the general election next preceding the expiration of the terms of their predecessors, except that the successors of the city magistrates heretofore appointed from the borough of Brooklyn and in office in the year nineteen hundred shall be elected at the election next preceding the expiration of their terms as hereinbefore designated, and they shall be elected at large in said borough of Brooklyn for the term of six years commencing on the first day of January succeeding their election, and their successors shall be elected for a like term and in a like manner. The successors to the present city magistrates for the boroughs of Queens and Richmond shall be elected at the general election to be held in said boroughs next preceding the expiration of their respective terms. At the general election to be held in the boroughs of Queens and Richmond in the year nineteen hundred and five there shall be elected in the territory constituting the borough of Queens, one city magistrate at large, and in the territory constituting the borough of Richmond one city magistrate at large, and at the general election to be held in the boroughs of Queens and Richmond in the year nineteen hundred and seven, there shall be elected in the territory constituting the borough of Queens, two city magistrates at large, and in the territory constituting the borough of Richmond one city magistrate at large. The terms of office of said city magistrates so elected for the boroughs of Queens and Richmond shall commence on the first day of January next succeeding their election and the terms of all said city magistrates so elected shall continue for six years thereafter. The successors of the said city magistrates in the boroughs of Queens and Richmond shall be elected for the like term and in the like manner at the general election next preceding the expiration of the terms of their successors. Upon the happening of any vacancy, the same shall be filled by election at the next general election occurring at least thirty days after such vacancy, at which an election for a city magistrate can be held. If such election is for an unexpired term, it shall be for the residue of said term, and until the first day of January next after such election, said office shall be filled by appointment by the mayor of The City of New York, within thirty days after such vacancy shall occur. The city magistrates elected or appointed pursuant to this act, shall, before entering upon their duties, take the oath of office prescribed by the constitution and file the same with the city clerk.

Police Clerks and employees.

§ 1394. The board of city magistrates of the first division

shall have the authority and duty of appointing seven police clerks [and the board for the second division shall have the authority and duty of appointing thirteen police clerks, and] each board shall regulate the time, place and manner of the discharge of the duty of the police clerks; but the police clerks in the first department* in office on the first day of January, nineteen hundred and two, shall continue to hold office until the expiration of their several terms. Each police clerk in the first department* shall be appointed for the term of four years, and, on making the appointment, the board shall cause three certificates to be signed by its president and secretary, each of which shall state the term of the office, the borough and division from which and the term for which the appointment is made, and when it will expire, and the secretary shall deliver one of said certificates to the person so appointed, and shall cause the other certificates to be filed, one in the office of the city clerk, and one in the office of the clerk of the county in which is situated the borough from which such person was appointed. Upon the question of the appointment of a police clerk or other appointee, in the first department* the members of the board shall vote as their names are called by the secretary, and the vote of each member shall be recorded in the minutes. [The salary of each police clerk in the first division, and in the borough of Brooklyn, shall be two thousand five hundred dollars, and in the boroughs of Queens and Richmond two thousand dollars a year, payable monthly, and no such] No clerk or other officer or employe appointed by a board of city magistrates, or by any magistrate,

*So in bill.

shall hold any other office or be interested in any other business, but they shall give their whole time to their respective duties, and shall be residents of The City of New York, and of the divisions within which they were appointed, and, in the second division, they shall each be residents of the borough from which they are appointed.

The police clerks and police clerks' assistants in office in said second division of The City of New York at the time this act takes effect shall continue in their respective offices until midnight of December thirty-first, nineteen hundred and one, after which date their respective duties shall cease and determine, and their different positions be deemed abolished.

Bond of police clerks.

§ 1395. Before any police clerk in the first division [appointed as provided in the preceding section,] shall enter upon the discharge of his duty, he shall file in the office of the comptroller of the city a bond in the penal sum of five thousand dollars, with two sureties, conditioned for the faithful discharge of his duty as a police clerk and the due accounting for and the payment of all money received by him as such clerk, such bond to be approved by said comptroller, whose approval shall be evidenced by his certificate endorsed thereon.

Other appointees.

§ 1396. The said boards of city magistrates [and each of them,] in the first division may appoint police clerks' assistants, stenographers, interpreters and other necessary attendants.

Such appointees, including those in office when this act takes effect, shall hold their respective positions so long as they are faithful, capable and of good conduct, and before removal, for want of either or all of said qualifications, the individual against whom charges are made shall have notice thereof, and an opportunity to make an explanation in the presence of the board, and the reasons for any removal shall be briefly entered in the minutes. The police clerks' assistants, and other assistants in any city magistrate's court, shall obey the reasonable directions of the police clerk assigned to that court, subject, however, to the proper orders of the city magistrate presiding and of the board of city magistrates. The number of police clerks' assistants in the first division shall not exceed fourteen [, and in the second division shall not exceed sixteen]. Police clerks' assistants in the boroughs of Manhattan and The Bronx shall receive a salary not exceeding two thousand dollars per annum. [; police clerks' assistants in the borough of Brooklyn shall receive a salary not exceeding fifteen hundred dollars per annum.] The salary of the stenographers shall not exceed, in the boroughs of Manhattan and Brooklyn, two thousand dollars per annum; in the other boroughs, eighteen hundred dollars per annum. [Any police clerks' assistants now in office beyond the number herein allowed shall be removed by the board of city magistrates]. There shall be no police clerks' assistants in the boroughs of Queens and Richmond, except as provided in the next section.

§ 1396a*. Each city magistrate hereafter elected in a congressional district or appointed for a full term in said second division of The City of New York shall have the authority to appoint one police clerk, and two assistant clerks and a stenographer, said clerks to perform such duties as the board of city magistrates in said second division shall regulate and determine. Each police clerk shall be appointed for the term of four years, and on making such appointments the city magistrate so appointing shall sign three certificates, each of which shall state the term of office, borough and division from which, and term for which, the appointment is made, and when it will expire. The magistrate shall deliver one of said certificates to the person so appointed, and shall cause the other certificates to be filed, one in the office of the city clerk, and one in the clerk's office of the county in which is situated the borough from which such person is appointed. The salary of each police clerk, in the first division and in the borough of Brooklyn, shall be twenty-five hundred dollars per annum, payable monthly, and the salary of each assistant clerk in the borough of Brooklyn shall not exceed two thousand dollars per annum, and in the boroughs of Queens and Richmond said clerks' salaries shall be two thousand dollars per year, payable monthly; and no such clerk, deputy clerk or employe appointed by said city magistrates shall hold any other office or be interested in any other business, but shall give their whole time to their respective duties, and shall be residents of the borough in which the appointing magistrate is elected.

*This section has no heading in bill.

From section 1397:—

Each board of city magistrates shall adopt, and may from time to time amend or add to, rules relating to the following subjects, and which shall be binding on said city magistrates, and shall regulate the business of such city magistrates*, courts and boards.

From section 1398:—

Subject to the rules which may be established for the holding of a part for the hearing of children's cases as provided in section thirteen hundred and ninety-nine, of this act, [a city magistrate shall be in constant attendance in each of the city magistrate's courts between the hours of nine o'clock in the morning and twelve o'clock noon, and between one o'clock and four o'clock in the afternoon on every day except Sundays and legal holidays, but including election day] the several city magistrates' courts shall be opened every day at nine o'clock in the morning, and in the first, second, third, fourth, fifth and seventh districts of the first division, and the first, second, third, fourth and fifth districts of the Borough of Brooklyn, shall not be closed before four o'clock in the afternoon, except on Saturdays, Sundays and holidays, when morning sessions only shall be necessary. The sixth district court of the first division, and each of said courts not above enumerated of the second division, shall be open each day during such hours as the respective boards of city magistrates shall by rule determine. On any day of general election each court shall be kept open until the polls are closed.

*So in bill.

From section 1401.

No person shall be appointed to the office of city magistrate unless he shall have been admitted to practice as an attorney and counsellor at law in the courts of this state at least five years prior to the date of such appointment, unless he was a police justice [be a city magistrate] in office on the first day of January, eighteen hundred and ninety-five [nineteen hundred and two.]

§ 1401a*. A city magistrate or police clerk may be removed for cause, after due notice and an opportunity of being heard, by the appellate division of the supreme court within the division for which such city magistrate or police clerk was appointed.

From section 1409:—

If a defendant desire to appeal from an order of filiation, mentioned in section eight hundred and fifty of the code of criminal procedure, such appeal shall be taken in accordance with section fourteen hundred and thirteen of this act, except that the presiding justice, or, in his absence or disability, any justice, who sat on the trial of the defendant may take a bond from the defendant in such sum and with such sureties as the said justice may approve, that he will abide the final decision of the appeal taken by him, and will pay all costs and disbursements on appeal, and that if the said order of filiation be affirmed he will obey it and make all the payments therein directed; and if the defendant is in custody, the justice may thereupon order

*This section has no heading in bill.

that the defendant be discharged from inprisonment and that all proceedings on the order of filiation be stayed pending the decision of the appeal therefrom. But a defendant who has executed an undertaking to obey an order of filiation and indemnify the public, as provided in section eight hundred and fifty-one of the code of criminal procedure, cannot appeal from any other part of said order than that which fixes the weekly or other allowance to be paid. If the said bond on appeal shall not be complied with it must be sued upon by the commissioner of public charities in whose jurisdiction it was given.

Duty of District attorney to attend court, etc.

§ 1415. It shall be the duty of the district attorney of each of the counties of New York, Kings, Queens and Richmond to attend in person or by an assistant at all sessions of said courts of special sessions within his county. [No district attorney or assistant district attorney of the counties of New York or Kings shall appear as attorney or counsel in any action or litigation, except in the discharge of his official duties, nor accept an appointment as referee or receiver in any action or proceeding.]

[TITLE 5.]

[*Interpreters.*]

[Interpreters.]

[§ 1430. The president of the municipal court justices, the president of the board of city magistrates of the first division, the president of the board of city magistrates of the second division, a justice of the court of special sessions of the first division to be selected by the justices of said court, and a justice of the court of special sessions of the second division to be selected by the justices of said court, shall constitute the board of control of interpreters for the inferior courts. All interpreters of the inferior courts of The City of New York other than The City Court of New York now in office, including those appointed pursuant to chapter six hundred and twenty-three of the laws of eighteen hundred and seventy-five, are hereby continued as such, and shall be subject to the control and supervision of said board of control, and shall report for duty in the court, or courts, to which they may be assigned by said board of control through the president thereof. Said board shall make rules and regulations governing the time and place of service of said interpreters and shall hold them amenable for any infraction of said rules, shall fill all vacancies and make removals for cause after due notice and hearing. The number of interpreters shall not exceed the number from time to time fixed by the board of aldermen on the recommendation of the board of estimate and apportionment. All vacancies in such position shall be filled by appointment by the board of control hereby created.]

§ 1436a*. It shall be the duty of the department board or officer which has selected lands as aforesaid to submit the matter to the board of estimate and apportionment, and no further proceedings shall be taken until the acquisition of said lands is approved and authorized by a majority vote of all the members of the said board of estimate and apportionment at a meeting of

*Number in bill is 143a. Section has no heading in bill.

said board duly called and held. Upon such authorization it shall be the duty of the corporation counsel to file in the office of the clerk of the county where the lands or any part thereof are situated a notice of the pendency of proceedings for the acquisition of said lands. The said notice shall briefly state the object of the proceedings and shall contain a description by metes and bounds of the property affected thereby. It shall also state the names of such of the persons interested as owners or otherwise as may be known to the corporation counsel, and in case any of such persons interested as owners or otherwise are unknown a statement to that effect shall be made in such notice. Such notice, from the time of filing, shall be constructive notice to a purchaser or incumbrancer of the lands affected thereby from or against any person interested as owner or otherwise with respect to whom the notice is directed to be indexed.

§ 1436b*. Said board of estimate and apportionment shall have power and is hereby authorized to agree as to the purchase price of the lands and interests therein selected as aforesaid or any part thereof. If no such agreement is reached, or if any such agreement does not include the whole of the lands and interest therein, the said board shall direct the corporation counsel to institute proceedings for the condemnation of said lands and interests therein or such part thereof in respect to which no agreement has been reached as aforesaid, and thereupon it shall be the duty of the corporation counsel to conduct proper proceedings thereunto in the manner provided in this chapter. When any agreement as to price has been reached as aforesaid

***This section is wrongly numbered 143b in bill.**

the amount agreed upon shall bear interest from the date of said agreement, and the time of vesting title in The City of New York to the lands affected by such agreement shall be the date of the delivery of the deed, and if no time be specified for the delivery of the deed title shall vest upon the date of the final confirmation of the report of commissioners, as hereinafter provided, as to property concerning which no agreement has been reached unless the date of vesting title is fixed by resolution as hereinafter provided.

§ 1436c. In all cases where the owner of lands selected as aforesaid or any part thereof is not under legal disability to convey title to real property such owner may at any time before proof of value is submitted to the commissioners of estimate hereinafter provided for, submit a written offer to the board of estimate and apportionment to sell and convey such owner's land or interest therein at a specified price. Such written offer shall not be given in evidence before the commissioners of estimate hereinafter provided for, and must not be considered by them. If such written offer is not accepted before proof of value is submitted to the commissioners of estimate hereinafter provided for, provided ten days shall have lapsed from the time of making such offer, and the compensation awarded thereafter in said proceedings by the commissioners of estimate to such person or owner making such offer exceeds the price specified in such offer such owner making such offer shall be entitled to his taxable costs and disbursements as in an action and in the discretion of the supreme court upon application made at a special term thereof to an additional allowance of a sum of money not exceeding five per centum upon the amount of such offer, but in no event more than two thousand dollars.

Appointment and duties of commissioners of estimate.

§ 1437. After the said maps, plans or surveys shall have been filed, and after the acquisition of the lands and interest therein shall have been authorized by the board of estimate and apportionment, as hereinbefore provided, the corporation counsel, for and or behalf of The City of New York, shall cause notice to be published in the City Record of his intention to make application to the supreme court for the appointment of commissioners of estimate and appraisal, which notice shall specify the time and place of such application, and shall briefly state the object of the application, and shall describe, generally, the lands intended to be taken. Said notice shall be published in ten successive issues of said City Record, and thereafter, upon the completion of such publication, said corporation counsel shall present to the court a petition, signed and verified by the mayor of said city, setting forth the action taken by the department, board or officer, with reference thereto, and the authorization of the proceedings, by a majority vote of all members of the board of estimate and apportionment, the filing of said map, plan or survey, and of a notice of the pendency of the proceeding, and praying for the appointment of such commissioners of estimate and appraisal. At the time and place mentioned in said notice, unless the said court shall adjourn the said application to a subsequent day, and in that event, at the time and place to which the same may be adjourned, the court, upon due proof to its satisfaction, of the publication of such notice, and upon filing the said petition, shall name three discreet and disinterested persons, being citizens of the United States, all of whom shall be residents of the borough where the property to be taken is located, as commissioners of estimate and appraisal for the purpose of performing the duties hereinafter mentioned. In such order the court shall fix the time and place for a hearing as to the qualifications of the persons named as commissioners. Ten days notice of the naming or appointment of the commissioners shall be given by the corporation counsel, by mail or otherwise, to such parties, or their attorneys, as may have filed a notice of claim or of appearance in the proceeding, and such notice shall be published in ten successive issues of the City Record. Said notice shall specify the time and place when parties may be heard at a special term of the supreme court, as to the qualifications of the persons named as commissioners of estimate and appraisal. The persons named as commissioners shall attend at the time and place appointed, and may be examined under oath, as to their qualifications to act. They shall be subject to the right of challenge by any person having an interest in said proceedings, upon any ground which would disqualify a judge or juror, and such challenge must be tried and determined by the court, and the determination of the court may be excepted to and reviewed in the manner now prescribed by law in respect to the challenge of jurors. Should the court sustain the challenge to any commissioner, another person must be named or appointed in his stead. The person or persons thus substituted shall be subject to challenge in the same way, as above provided for, to be heard and determined by the court, at such time and place as the court may direct.

§ 1437a. The persons finally appointed commissioners of estimate and appraisal, after the trial and determination of any challenge, as hereinbefore provided, shall severally take and subscribe an oath or affirmation as prescribed by the thirteenth article of the constitution of this state, and shall forthwith file the same in the office of the clerk of the supreme court in the judicial district in which said lands are situated, and thereupon it shall be the duty of the said commissioners of estimate and appraisal, after having viewed the said lands, tenements, hereditaments and premises required for public uses and purposes, as above set forth, to make a just and equitable estimate of the loss and damage to the respective owners, lessees, parties or persons respectively entitled to or interested in the said lands, tenements, hereditaments and premises. But no meeting of such commissioners shall be held at the office of the corporation counsel, or at the office of any party interested in the proceeding, or in the office of the attorney of any such party interested. [When the said maps, surveys or plans have been filed as hereinbefore provided, the said department board or officer of the said city acting by and through the corporation counsel of said city, is hereby authorized to make application to a special term of the supreme court, in and for the judicial district in which said lands are situated, for the appointment of commissioners of estimate, and the said court shall thereupon name three discreet and disinterested persons, being residents of The City of New York, as such commissioners of estimate, for the purpose of performing the duties hereinafter mentioned. Ten days' notice of such application, Sundays and holidays excluded, shall be published in the City Record, and the corporation newspapers and also at the option of the corporation counsel in other newspapers, nbt exceeding three in number, published in said City of New York. Upon the appointment of said commissioners they shall severally take and subscribe an oath or affirmation, before some officer authorized to administer oaths, in the form required by section one of article thirteen of the constitution of this state, which oaths shall be forthwith filed in the office of the clerk of the supreme court in the judicial district in which said lands are situated. It shall be the duty of the said commissioners, after having viewed the said lands, tenements, hereditaments and premises required for public uses and purposes, as above set forth, to make a just and equitable estimate of the loss and damage to the respective owners, lessees, parties and persons respectively entitled to or interested in the said lands, tenements, hereditaments and premises, and to make report thereof to the said supreme court with due diligence.]

Reports of commissioners of estimate; presentation thereof to the court; when title to vest in city.

§1438. The said commissioners of estimate and appraisal shall make report of their proceedings to the supreme court, with the minutes of the testimony taken by them, and with the minutes of the proceedings, if any, relating to the challenge of any commissioner, within six months from the date of the filing of their oath, as hereinbefore provided, under penalty of forfeiting all fees to which they would be entitled, unless an extension of time be given to them by the supreme court, which extension shall only be granted in the discretion of the court, upon a written petition containing a full statement by such commissioners, of the reasons necessary for such an extension, and upon notice to the corporation counsel, and to the parties, and their attorneys who have appeared in said proceeding. Upon such application the court shall have power to make such order in the premises in respect to the time and manner of completing the report of such commissioners, and in respect to the taking and submission of the proofs of the parties interested, and the number and length of the hearings to be held in each week as will enable or require the commissioners to complete said proceedings on their part with reasonable despatch, and if it shall appear that the said proceeding has been delayed, by reason of the inattention, neglect or refusal of said commissioners or any of them, to act or attend, the court may remove the commissioner or commissioners so neglecting or refusing, and appoint a suitable person or persons in his or their place. Said report shall contain a brief description of the several parcels of real estate taken, with a reference to the map, plan or survey, showing the exact location and boundaries of each parcel, a statement of the sum estimated and determined upon by them as a just and equitable compensation to be made by the city, to the owners or persons entitled or interested in each parcel so taken, and a statement of the respective owners or persons entitled thereto or interested therein. But in all and each and every case or cases, where the parties interested, or their respective estates or interests, are unknown or are not fully known to the commissioners of appraisal it shall be sufficient for them to set forth and state, in general terms, the respective sums to be allowed and paid to the owners of and parties interested therein, generally, without specifying the names or estates or interests of such owners or parties interested, or any or either of them. After the commissioners shall have offered the parties interested an opportunity to file and make objections as provided for in section fourteen hundred and forty, then the said report, signed by said commissioners or a majority of them, shall be filed in the office of the department, board or officer, initiating the proceeding, and a duplicate of said report shall be filed in the office of the corporation counsel, and thereupon the corporation counsel, or in case of his neglect to do so within ten days after such filing, then any interested in the proceeding shall give notice that the said report will be presented for confirmation to the supreme court, at a special term thereof, to be held in the City of New York, at a time and place to be specified in said notice. The said notice shall contain a statement of the time and place of the filing of the report, and shall be published in ten successive issues of the City Record, immediately prior to the presentation of said report for confirmation, and a copy of said notice shall be served, by mail or otherwise, upon the attorney of each party who may have appeared in said proceeding, at least five days prior to the presentation of said report for confirmation. [In each and all and every case when the owners, or parties interested, or their respective estates and interests are unknown, or not fully known, to the said commissioners, it shall be sufficient for them to estimate and set forth and state in their said reports, in general terms, the respective sums to be allowed and paid to the owners and proprietors generally of such lands, tenements, hereditaments and premises and parties interested therein, for the loss and damage to such owners, proprietors and parties interested in respect of the whole estate and interest of whomsoever may be entitled unto or interested in said lands, tenements, hereditaments and premises respectively, by and in consequence of the taking of the same, as herein provided, without specifying the names of the estate or interests of such owners, proprietors, and parties interested, or either of them, and upon the coming in]

§ 1438a. Upon the hearing of the application for the confirmation of the said report, signed by the said commissioners, or a majority of them, the said supreme court at a special term thereof held in and for the judicial district as aforesaid, shall, by order, upon application of the said city, or the said department or board of the government thereof conducting said proceeding, after hearing any matter which may be alleged against the same, either confirm said report in whole or in part or refer the same back to the same commissioners for revisal and correction, or to new commissioners, to be appointed by the said court.

§ 1438b. It shall be the duty of the corporation counsel, within ten days after the entry of the order confirming the report of the commissioners, in a proceeding authorized by this chapter to file a copy of such order or report in the office of the register or county clerk of the county in which the land to be acquired is located. There shall be endorsed upon such copy order or report a referee to the section and block or the sections and blocks on the land map of such county which include the land to be taken by such proceeding. The register or county clerk with whom such copy order or report shall be filed shall index in the index of conveyances on each block so endorsed on the said copy order or report, a statement giving the title of said proceeding and the date of the entry of said order confirming said report.

From section 1439:—Should the board of estimate and apportionment by a resolution adopted by a three-fourths vote [department board or officer of the said city government instituting the said proceeds] deem it for the public interest that the title to the lands and premises, or any interest therein, required for any public improvement or for any public purpose and acquired hereunder, should be acquired by The City of New York at a fixed or specified time, the said [department board or officer] board of estimate and apportionment may direct, by resolution passed before the application to the court for the appointment of commissioners of estimate, made under section fourteen hundred and thirty-seven of this act, [if said resolution be approved by the board of estimate and apportionment by a three fourths vote,] and [which said resolution [and approval] shall be recited in the petition for the appointment of such commissioners], that at a date specified in such resolution [four months] after the filing of the oaths of said commissioners, the title to any piece or parcel of land, or to any interest therein, to be taken or acquired in the said proceeding, shall vest in The City of New York. * * * * [At the expiration of said four months from the filing of said oaths,] the said City of New York shall become and be seized in fee of said City of New York shall become and be seized in fee of said land tenements and hereditaments. * * * * And [at the expiration of the said four months and] upon the vesting of said title, the said city, acting by and through the said department board or officer conducting said proceeding, shall immediately take possession of the lands included in the same and the interests thereby affected, without any suit or proceeding at law for that purpose.

From section 1440.—The said commissioners of estimate, at least fourteen days before they present their report to the supreme court, shall deposit a true report or transcript of such estimate in the office of the department or board or officer conducting such proceeding, for the inspection of whomsoever it may concern, and shall give daily notice by advertisement in the City Record and the corporation newspapers, and also, at the option of the corporation counsel, in other newspapers, not exceeding three in number, published in said City of New York, for ten days, Sundays and holidays excluded, after depositing such report, of the said deposit thereof in said office, [and for the day on which the said report will be presented to said court.] * * * * The City of New York shall, within two calendar months after the confirmation of the said report, pay to the parties entitled thereto the respective sum or sums so estimated and reported in their favor, respectively, with lawful interest from the date of [the confirmation of] the report of said commissioners, or if title to said lands shall have vested in the city under section fourteen hundred and thirty-nine of this act, from the date of said vesting.

Corporation counsel to appear and protect interests of city. Comptroller to furnish clerks and office.

§ 1446. The corporation counsel shall, either in person, or by such counsel as he shall designate for the purpose, appear for and protect the interests of the city in all such proceedings in court and before the commissioners of estimate. It shall be the duty of the comptroller of The City of New York to furnish the commissioners of estimate and appraisal who may be appointed in any proceeding provided for in this chapter such necessary clerks and other employes and to provide such suitable offices as they may require to enable them to fully and satisfactorily discharge the duties imposed upon them.

From section 1447 :—

The said proof shall be made by a statement duly verified in which shall be set forth in addition to other matters required by law and practice the respective dates of the rendition of services, and in the case of commissioners, and of any clerks who may receive a per diem allowance, the number of hours or the time necessarily occupied upon each of such respective dates. And no such claim for compensation shall be taxed, allowed or paid unless it be accompanied by a certificate of the comptroller of the city of New York setting forth that the same has been audited and examined, and further certifying the result of such audit and examination.

CHAPTER XXII.

Stages and omnibuses; consents of property owners necessary before franchise granted.

Section 1458. No stage or omnibus route, or authority to run stages or omnibuses in The City of New York, shall hereafter be granted by the board of aldermen, unless a majority of the owners of property upon the streets in or upon which any such route or privilege is to be operated, shall before the board of aldermen act on the subject, first consent in writing thereto.

Application to mayor, etc.: before route established.

§ 1459. Before any route for the running of omnibuses or stages shall be established or allowed to be operated in said city, except as provided in this act, the application therefor shall be made in writing to the mayor of said city, specifying the route proposed to be established and the number of stages or omnibuses proposed to be run thereon; and unless the said mayor shall communicate such application to the board of aldermen with his approval thereof, and said board of aldermen, after receiving such communication and approval, shall vote in favor thereof by a three-fourths vote of all the members, no such route shall be established or operated; and upon such favorable action such route may be established and operated accordingly and the ownership thereof may be transferred.

Stage route to be disposed of like other franchises.

§ 1460. Any stage route or privilege hereafter granted by the board of aldermen shall be disposed of in the manner provided by law for the disposition of the franchises of said city.

Not to be run except in conformity with preceding sections or as hereinafter provided.

§ 1461. It shall not be lawful to run stages or omnibuses in The City of New York, as constituted by this act, except in conformity with the preceding sections, and no stage route shall, after April first, nineteen hundred and one, be established or operated upon that portion of any street, avenue, road or highway in which a street surface railway or stage route is or shall be lawfully established, and in operation for a distance greater than one thousand feet, without first obtaining the consent of the corporation owning such railway or stage route, but nothing in this act shall be constructed to affect the right possessed by any company to operate stage routes or extensions then established and in lawful operation, nor to affect any authority conferred upon any such company to acquire rights and privileges under chapter six huudred and fifty-seven of the laws of nineteen hundred, nor to affect any acts heretofore done thereunder.

The bill would repeal sections 1510 to 1520, both inclusive, relating to the board of pharmacy and the registration of pharmacists.

From section 1526:—

There shall be published daily, Sundays and legal holidays excepted, under a contract to be made as hereinafter provided, a paper to be known as the City Record. And said City Record, and the newspapers now by law designated as corporation newspapers in the present city of Brooklyn, and those that shall be designated as hereinafter provided in the boroughs of The Bronx, Queens and Richmond, shall be the only papers to be included within the term corporation newspapers as the same is used anywhere in this act; but no notice or advertisement shall be inserted in any of said newspapers in said city of Brooklyn, nor in such as shall be designated as hereinafter provided, in the boroughs of The Bronx, Queens and Richmond, except such as respect matters exclusively occurring within or relating to the borough [of Brooklyn exclusively] in which any such newspaper is published; and the aggregate amount to be paid to said newspapers now designated by law as corporation newspapers, in said city of Brooklyn, or hereafter designated as hereinafter provided, in each of said boroughs of Queens, Richmond and Bronx, for the publication of all advertisements provided for by this act, in each of said boroughs respectively, shall never exceed in any year, the sum now agreed to be paid [to said newspapers] annually by said city of Brooklyn to said newspapers now by law designated as corporation newspapers in said city of Brooklyn. In addition to said City Record and said newspapers now designated by law in said city of Brooklyn, there shall be four corporation papers in the borough Queens and two corporation papers in each of the boroughs of the Bronx and Richmond. It shall be the duty of the mayor of The City of New York, as soon as this act shall take effect, to designate four publications in the borough of Queens and two publications in each of the said boroughs of The Bronx and Richmond, to be known as such corporation papers for the term of four years from the date of such designation and, respectively, until their successors are designated; two of said publications in the borough of Queens and one of said publications in each of said boroughs of The Bronx and Richmond, so to be designated by the mayor of The City of New York, shall be selected by the chairman of the borough committee, if there be such a committee; otherwise, by the chairman of the county committee of the county in which the borough is located, of the party casting at the last preceding general election the greatest number of votes within the state for the head of the state ticket, and two, within said borough of Queens and one, within each of the said boroughs of The Bronx and Richmond, shall be selected by the chairman of the borough committee, if there be such a committee; otherwise, by the chairman of the county committee of the county within which the borough is located, of the party casting at the last preceding general election the next greatest number of votes within the state for the head of the state ticket; and the mayor of the City of New York must take such designations as shall be so selected and presented to him by said chairman, respectively, and every notice and advertisement relating exclusively to a particular borough, shall be published in the newspapers so selected and published within such borough. Such publications so designated shall be printed and published in daily form and shall have been published for at least sixty days prior to this act becoming a law, in a daily form within the borough of Queens, and in either a weekly, semi-weekly or daily form, within the said boroughs of The Bronx and Richmond.* * * * * * * and where such notices and advertisements respect matters occurring within or relating to the borough of Brooklyn, they shall also be published in such newspapers as are now by law designated as corporation newspapers in the City of Brooklyn, and where such notices and advertisements respect matters occurring or relating to either the borough of The Bronx, Queens or Richmond, they shall also be published in the corporation newspapers within the borough to which said advertisements relate as shall have been designated as herein provided, for such borough, and each of said publications within the said boroughs of Brooklyn, Bronx, Queens and Richmond, shall, respectively, receive the rates of payment therefor, equal to but not to exceed the compensation now paid to said newspapers within the borough of Brooklyn for like advertisements in the City of Brooklyn, of county of Kings.

From section 1543:—

But no regular clerk or head of a bureau, or person holding a position in the classified municipal civil service subject to competitive examination, shall be removed until he has been allowed an opportunity of making an explanation; and in every case of a removal, the true grounds thereof shall be forthwith entered upon the records of the department or board or borough president, and copy filed with the municipal civil service.* In case of removal, a statement showing the reason therefor shall be filed in the department.

From section 1570:—

Two coroners shall hereafter be elected in the borough of Manhattan, two in the borough of The Bronx, two in the borough of Brooklyn, [one] two in the borough of Queens and one in the borough of Richmond.

* So in bill.

www.ingramcontent.com/pod-product-compliance
Lightning Source LLC
LaVergne TN
LVHW021429110826
845150LV00007B/2158